CEREDIGION
FOLK
TALES

T0333473

CEREDIGION
FOLK
TALES

PETER STEVENSON

The
History
Press

'There's one advantage in being poor.
It's very inexpensive.'

– Ceredigion proverb

First published 2014

The History Press
The Mill, Brimscombe Port
Stroud, Gloucestershire, GL5 2QG
www.thehistorypress.co.uk

Reprinted 2017

British Library Cataloguing in Publication Data.
A catalogue record for this book is available from the British Library.

ISBN 978 0 7524 8644 4

Typesetting and origination by The History Press
Printed in Great Britain by TJ Books Ltd, Padstow, Cornwall.

CONTENTS

Acknowledgements

Thanks to Declan Flynn and Chris Ogle at The History Press, the National Library of Wales, Emma Lile at the National History Museum at St Fagans, Robin Gwyndaf for allowing access to his archive, Lucy Thomas at the Welsh Books Council, Stuart Evans, Jez Danks, and Anna Evans at Ceredigion Museum, Helen and Anya at Ceredigion Archive, Catrin at the National Sound Archive, the librarians of Ceredigion, Emily Trahair and *Planet* magazine, Gill Ogden and Aberystwyth Arts Centre, Cecil Sharp House, Fiona Collins, Dafydd Eto and David Moore, Ceri Owen-Jones, Elsa Davies, Iola Billings, Dafydd Wyn Morgan, Mary-Ann Constantine, Valériane Leblond, Bethan Miles, Conti's café, Yarn Storytellers, Delyth and Dafydd at Ty Mawr, Jonathan Davies, Gerald Morgan, Gordon Jones, Mabel Pakenham-Walsh, Chris Grooms, Sue Clow, Michael Freeman, Derek Bryce, Jen Jones and the Welsh Quilt Centre, Tony and Cory Mortis-Wait, Martin at Ystwyth Books, Hazel Thomas at the People's Collection Wales, Brian Swaddling, Linda and Sarah in the Print Shop at NLW, Kevin Williams, Peter Jones, Bob the poet, Susan Passmore, Anthony Morris, Alan Hale, and to all the little red mannikins, one-eyed preachers, transvestite ghosts, *dyn hysbys*, drunken mermaids, mischievous *bwcas*, headless dogs, two-headed calves, expired elephants and long-nosed fiddlers who have taken the time to indulge a curious gentleman of the road and have invited him to drink water from oak leaves rolled into the shape of a cone.

INTRODUCTION

FOLK TALES AND STORYTELLING IN CEREDIGION

Myra Evans was born in New Quay in 1883. She was a writer, a storyteller, an illustrator, a mother of six, a linguist, a humanist, a teacher, a collector of music, songs and lullabies, and a singer, although she considered herself more a crow than a canary. She learned fairy tales from her family and friends: from her father Thomas Rees of 'Glasfryn', her grandfather Rees Rees, and her great grandfather Daniel Williams of 'Glyngolau'; from the old sea captains David Jones of 'Annie Brocklebank' and Captain Davies 'Loch Shiels' and a cobbler, William Evans.

Myra left us a jewel, a collection of fairy tales and local legends, each of them about named people and places, dating from before the 1850s. They are misty memories of local characters, and of farmhouses and cottages, some now in ruins while others have 4x4s on tarmac driveways and Laura Ashley drapes in PVC windows. Often there are caravan parks, though the streams still sing their harmonies to the grey wagtails and the overhanging oak trees.

These stories are of another world, an Otherworld so familiar to the folk of Ceredigion 100 years ago; exotic and enticing, dark and dangerous, curious and comical, a world of the marginalised and misunderstood, of flooded lands and lost languages. A dreamworld.

Myra's stories reflect the entwining of the landscape and its people. Telling tales is part of the richness of conversation, language, poetry, humour, metaphor and banter in Ceredigion.

Stories were often only known within families or small communities, always told in Welsh at informal gatherings in the kitchen, having first ensured to invite the old farmer who knew all the tittle tattle, and the young woman who played all her *taid's* (grandad's) tunes on the fiddle he had given her when she was 5. Along with the storytellers there were singers, musicians, gossips, dancers, poets, quilters, carpenters, preachers and teachers; often they were all the same person. There was the woman with her jars of herbal remedies, and the conjurer, the *dyn hysbys*, with his recitations, incantations and his book of spells, a source of fear and not a little amusement to many a child. This was a world where every girl and boy were expected from an early age to perform. There were plenty of opportunities at social gatherings: the *Noson Lawen*, the merry nights in the village halls which celebrated the harvest; the *Pilnos*, when folk gathered to make rush lights, passing the long night with stories and songs, and the local *Eisteddfodau*, the annual competitions organised to encourage the creative arts, and to decide who should represent the village at the national event.

The folk poets, *y bardd gwylad*, were articulate, intelligent, intuitive artists who could express emotions and stories in verse, in strict metre or less formally, giving a voice to those who did not have their command of language. The boys of Cilie farmhouse just north of Llangrannog were well renowned as wordsmiths. Saunders Lewis' description of the folk poets applies equally to the storytellers:

> The folk poet was a craftsman or farmer who followed his occupation in the area where he was born, who knew all the people in the neighbourhood and who could trace their family connections, who also knew the dialect of his native heath, and every story, event and omen, and who used the traditional social gift of poetry to console a bereaved family, to contribute to the jollifications at a wedding feast, or to record a contretemps with lightly malicious satire. His talent was a normal part of the propriety and entertainment of the Welsh rural society, chronicling its happenings, adorning its walls and its tombstones, recording its characters, its events, its sadness and its joy. It was a craft, the metres, the vocabulary,

the praise and the words of courtesy were traditional. It was not expected that it should be different from its kind. It was sufficient that it appropriately followed the pattern ... The kin of these poets are the mountain birds, the rainbow and the lonely places. They do not marry or give in marriage, they do not quarrel, and do not see their neighbours often enough to be satirical about them.

Cerngoch, a farmer from Bronant at the end of the nineteenth century, divided his work into these categories: nature, love, doorstep, beer, hunting, to persons, memorial, moral, force of habit, hypocrisy, the virtuous woman, religion, trivia and *englynion* (structured poetry).

These small farming and fishing communities on the windswept fringe of western Britain are not as isolated as some believe. News hawkers, itinerant puppeteers, magic lantern showmen, theatrical troupes, musicians, tramps, travelling menageries, broadsheet and chapbook sellers, seasonal agricultural workers who moved from farm to farm, all of them travellers, brought tales with them. Ships docked along the coast, bringing sailors and smugglers from all over the world, each with a story to tell; the Gypsies settled on either side of the Dyfi estuary and told stories reminiscent of the *Arabian Nights* or eastern European wonder tales; Margaret Jones, illustrator of *Tales from the Mabinogion* (ed. Jones, Gwyn & Kevin Crossley-Holland [London: Victor Gollancz, 1984]) performed her puppet shows in her homes in Tre Taliesin and India; a couple of hundred years ago Cornishmen came to work in the lead mines; in the 1930s Italians fleeing poverty came up from South Wales and opened cafes; Poles fled mainland Europe during the war and opened delis; students came from all over the world to study at the universities in Aberystwyth and Lampeter. The county has always been independent and free-thinking, and a few years ago boasted the gay and lesbian capital of Wales. They say of Aberystwyth that most of the country celebrates one queen, whereas Aber celebrates them all. Preachers travelled the land telling tales, much as some storytellers preach. Within the last fifty years the English language storytellers have arrived, following on from the New Age settlers in the early 1970s. They have brought with them new ideas of storytelling as an environmental tool, as performance theatre, as an expression of women's beliefs, and as a means to heal body and soul.

Given the ever-changing nature of traditions and communities, all a book like this can do is to offer a snapshot of stories from a moment of time. Ceredigion has been my home for twenty years, walking the old Welsh tramping roads with a sketchbook and an open ear, listening to stories over mugs of black tea and lemon cake in corner cafés, and vanishing into manuscripts and books in archives and libraries as a fiddler would step into a fairy ring. There are no stories from the Mabinogion here, as few are specifically set in Ceredigion, and they can easily be read elsewhere. Pryderi was King of Dyfed, though his court was further south than Ceredigion, Cei and Bedwyr sat on Pumlimon before they plucked the hair from the giant's beard, and Gwydion marched the enchanted pigs he had stolen from Pryderi back through the county. Perhaps the Mabinogion owes rather more to literature than folklore, although its stories are now a fundamental part of the repertoire of Welsh storytellers. A storyteller in Borth illustrates the tale with the tattoos on his arm as he rolls up his sleeve. Rhiannon, Branwen and Blodeuwedd in five minutes, with pictures.

Ceredigion is a land of contrasts, where old meets new, where dolphins swim close to the biggest fish-processing plant in the land; where men dress in women's clothes not only for a Friday night out with the boys, but to stand up for their liberty and carry out acts of subversion; where conjurers weave their spells in the hills away from those who think they wear pointy hats, cloaks, long grey beards and appear on Saturday night TV; where the last beavers in Wales lived on the banks of the Teifi rather than in a cage waiting for permission to be released as part of a reintroduction scheme; and where the fair folk are darker and more dangerous than the gossamer-winged sprites who live in the illustrations in children's picture books. It is a land where people speak the language of story, and the stories have mud on their boots.

MARI BERLLAN
PITTER

There is a young man, one of those gaunt, earnest young men, with bottle-bottom glasses, unruly fair hair, a book under his arm, and a thermos strapped to a rucksack on his back. He's looking for remains, antiquities, stories from the past, with mud on his boots and bramble scratches on his legs. He's thirsty from walking but too nervous to ask for water in the pub in Pennant, as it was a little rowdy. He's passing an old farmhouse, Mynachdy, and as he reaches the gate, he is wondering whether to ask for a drink, when a girl limps out in front of him. She's dark, jet-black hair flecked with red, deep dark eyes full of pain, and thin red lips that seem to be spitting blood. Plain and pretty at the same time, he thinks, for he is just at that difficult age. She has a slight hunch to her shoulder, head wrapped in a shawl, and hobnailed boots against bare legs. She is burning fury. She turns to look back at the entrance to the farm where the man is standing, and a stream of venom pours from her mouth. His Welsh is poor, though he understands enough to know that this is not kindly meant. She stares him in the eye, he is rooted to the spot, and he doesn't know if he is terrified or in love. But in the blink of a crow's eye, she's gone.

He looks around, and on the road towards Cilau Aeron he sees a hare, watching him. One of those ancient scarred hares that can outstare a lurcher. It runs into a field and follows the line of an old thorn hedge, weaving in and out like dog rose and honeysuckle, unscratched by the blackthorn and bramble. He follows, running along the line of the hedge. It's so thickly woven; how could a hare pass through it? When he is one side of the hedge, the hare is on the other, he climbs over gates and fences, rusting wire tearing his shirt, bruising his leg, trapping fingers, squelching through cow pats. He is in a thorn thicket, his trousers ripped, knees torn, mud mingling with blood. He pulls himself out, and there is the hare, in a circle where a castle once stood, staring at him. It turns and disappears down a bank; he follows, slips on his backside, bangs the back of his head on a stone, and sits there with his boots dangling in the stream.

On the opposite bank is the hare. Their eyes meet. It's laughing at him. It turns and runs up the wooded slope through a carpet of wild garlic, towards a cottage built into the rock face, pretty and double-fronted, smoke billowing from tall chimneys that look like rabbit's ears. He watches the hare run through a patch of strawberries in the garden and in through the front door. He picks himself up, wades across the river and up to the cottage. He hears a voice, 'Dewch i mewn, cariad.' A woman's voice. 'Don't be shy, take off your boots.' He does, and walks in.

The room is sepia and ochre, full of smoke and smells that tickle his nose, sweet and sour, aromatic and leafy, like cooking herbs. The walls are covered in sagging shelves and oak cabinets, full of misty brown jars and green glass bottles. There is an inglenook at one end, surrounded by a wickerwork screen, with dried bryony and wormwood hanging from the lintel. Sat in a worn rocking chair is an old woman, stirring a black pot hanging from a hook and chain over the open fire. She is small, grey hair flecked with black, deep dark eyes, thin white lips, and a wrinkled round face wrapped in a shawl that covers a slight hump on one shoulder. There is no sign of the hare. She ladles out the contents of the cauldron into a bowl and holds it out to him.

'There's bara brith on the table, fill your belly. You're as thin as a rake.' She looks him up and down. 'You've made a mess of yourself, my boy. Sit down, pull down your trousers and we'll bathe those cuts.' He can't refuse. She fetches bottles and jars and mixes potions and powders and, with a small piece of red muslin, she cleans the mud from his wounds and fills them with concoctions and tinctures. She asks him what he is doing in the woods, and he explains: antiquities, folk tales, old characters, you know. She knows, and while she cleans his cuts, she tells him stories, as if she understands exactly what he is seeking.

The cottage, she says, is Berllan Pitter, the Bitter Orchard. A family lived here 200 years ago; John and Mary Davies, with their daughter Mari and son David. Father worked at the big house, Mynachdy, as a gardener. Mynachdy was haunted by a ghost so small it could pass through the eye of a needle. Mari started working there too, as a maidservant. She was one of those dark intense girls, strong-willed and sensitive, mending broken animals, always seeing phantoms, pulling the heads from dolls, invoking spirits. She loved horses; she could whisper to them, send them to sleep, just like the man at Strata Florida. When her parents died, she was turned 50, set in her ways. She had fallen out with a man at the big house long ago, so had to earn a living for herself. She turned to the plants in the woods and became an herbalist. And so the stories started.

She was regarded as a little odd, away with the fairies; fine when you're young and nearly pretty, but when you get older, well, curtains twitch and fingers point. She had a wicked sense of humour. People would ask her, 'What you been

doin' today, Mari?' and she would answer, 'Drownin' kittens.'
She started visiting people, selling her potions and remedies,
asking for money or food in exchange. Many had known her father
and took pity on her, and if they refused, she simply turned and
walked away with her head down, without a word. Sometimes she
cursed them, under her breath, or loudly if they were objection-
able. People started to believe that her curses came true. Animals
fell ill, people too; butter wouldn't churn; she cursed three farmers
and they all lost cattle; she made a young girl walk backwards;
she turned Dic Roderick's water wheel at Llanarth into reverse,
and horses wouldn't pass her house because she'd put a protective
spell on it. Even her own cousin's horse stood stock still until she
lifted her curse. Only one man was safe from her spells: Lluestwr,
the local poet. Not only could she curse, she could lift the spells of
others. She would place a ball of wool in a bowl of water, stick a
pin into it and recite a chapter of the Bible, for she was a devout
chapel goer. They said she had power, fear spread, and soon the
word witchery was heard, which made her curse even more.

Witchcraft was known all over Ceredigion. Young girls made
potions to attract men, cure animals and heal wounds. There were
stories about Pegi Jonin in Bronant, Black Ellen the Gypsy of
Gogerddan, Beti Grwca of New Quay, Beti Havard of Llangybie,
and Crick y Wheel of Llanbadarn Fawr who dug up vegetables and
milked cows in the middle of the night and threatened to break
people's heads with a sickle if they came near. Her daughter sup-
posedly had a crooked eye which could bewitch you just by staring.
There were three witches in Aberarth who could make themselves
disappear and reappear in Cardigan. A servant at Dolfawr laughed
at the idea that Betty'r Bont of Ystrad Meurig had powers, until one
night he found he had been turned into a hare and was chased all
the way to bed by two greyhounds. Another night she turned him
into a horse, saddled him and rode him till dawn. In Llangwyryfon
in 1922 a woman cursed a cow, which promptly sat down, refused
to move and had to be shot. At Lluest Farm in Llwyngroes, an old
woman cursed a farmer who refused her food, and all his pigs lay
on their backs with their trotters in the air. In Talybont a woman

was thought to have turned herself into a hare, while in Llandre one was shot when in the form of a hare. A woman from Tregaron asked a farmer's wife for a small corner of his large farm to grow some potatoes, but was turned away from the door by a servant. The servant saw a hare looking at him, assumed it was the woman, took a gun and shot at her, but the hare ran away. Friends told him that she could only be killed by a bent fourpenny silver coin. He shot at the hare again, it rolled over screaming terribly, and the old woman was found later with a wound. The doctor was sent for and he found a bent fourpenny silver coin in two pieces embedded in her leg. He called her a witch, refused to treat her and she died.

If there were witches, there were also charms and protections against them. In Bettws Bledrws a woman tried to steal a horse but failed because it wore a protective necklace known as *Ialen Cerddenin*; a man in Lledrod asked the local conjuror for a written charm after being bewitched by a hag; there were snakestones, round stones thought to be formed when the heads of two snakes met; witch bottles, half-filled with lead, designed to hold her spirit which were then buried beneath a yew tree; in Ysbyty Ystwyth, a couple smeared fungus on a gatepost to protect themselves against a witch, and in Llanafan, a workman found witch's butter on the shafts of a wagon, which he scraped off and burned, thinking that would also kill the witch.

They could cure, too. Up until the late 1920s a woman in Aberystwyth had cured dozens of people of disease of the heart, *clefyd y galon*, by measuring their heads with a piece of yarn and mixing a drink made of brandy and yellow cake saffron. An old woman in Mynydd Bach a hundred years earlier cured a young woman of love by placing her by a tub of water and molten lead. Indigestion was cured by herbs boiled in urine, and rickets by snipping the ear.

The young man has been listening intently, but his memory is poor and he's cursing himself for not recording all this. He looks at his legs and the wounds are almost healed, the bruising gone from his arms; she's even sewed the rips in his trousers. He thanks her and offers her a piece of chocolate but she refuses, saying a young girl like her must look after her teeth. 'Wouldn't want to turn into an old hag. People would talk.' He takes up his rucksack, and she says, 'I'll tell you what started all this. Mari – when she was young and darkly pretty – one of the squires at the big house took a fancy to her. Kensington, his name. They had a bit of a hoo-ha, well, you know. Then he dumped her, threw her out. She walked out the front gate, turned round and cursed him. She was burning fury. History says she was a witch who died in 1898, carried to her grave in a cart pulled by a horse she'd cursed. Folk say she had a daughter; they went to live in Llanarth, where she died in 1904. There are lots of truths, my boy.'

He leaves and scrambles to the top of the bank, and looks down at the little cottage in the orchard. Berllan Pitter is as it has been ever since Mari left. A ruin.

In the 1980s, Theatr Felinfach were producing a show on Mari's life, and rehearsals went so badly that the cast went to the ruins of her house and buried a script there to pacify her. In 2006 a BBC film crew were at Llyn Tegid, looking for Teggie the lake creature for a series called *Celtic Monsters*. Filming was affected by a large hornet who attacked Neville Hughes, a BBC employee. The story made the *Western Mail* because Mr Hughes said the hornet was Mari, who often used to shapeshift. A crude attempt at publicity, the media's overblown ideas of their own importance, a joke that took on a life of its own? Or had Mari flown all the way up to Snowdonia as a hornet specifically to annoy the BBC? They were right about one thing; Mari was known for shapeshifting, often taking the form of a hare to mislead gullible young men.

Sir Dafydd Llwyd,
the Conjurer of Ceredigion

In *Itinerarium Cambriae* (1191), a description of his tour of Wales three years previously, Giraldus Cambrensis describes meeting soothsayers who when consulted go into a trance, lose control of their senses as if they are possessed, speak apparently meaningless words which suggest answers to your problems, and have to be violently shaken to wake them. Gerald is describing conjurers, *dynion hysbys*, cunning men. There have been many in Ceredigion, some charismatic, others solitary, all working their magic in very different ways, and all with their books of spells and written remedies. John Harries of Cwrt-y-Cadno served much of the south of the county early in the nineteenth century, Evan Griffiths from

Llangurig oversaw the north, and there were others from Pencader, Talybont, Goginan, Trefechan and Ponterwyd. Then there was Sir Dafydd Llwyd of Ysbyty Ystwyth.

Sir Dafydd lived in the early eighteenth century. He was a clergyman who learned the Black Arts when in Oxford, which lead to him being defrocked by the bishop, taking the title of Sir, and moving to Ysbyty Ystwyth. He had a book of spells where he kept his familiar, a demon which shapeshifted and assisted him in his art. He had no rivals, and there is no description of him, which only adds to his mystique. A conjurer from Lampeter once challenged him to a battle of the Black Arts, to demonstrate their control over demons. On the appointed morning, Sir Dafydd arrived early and sent his young apprentice boy to the top of the hill to watch the road from Lampeter. The boy was eager to please, and aware of what might happen to him if he didn't obey. He scampered up the hill and saw a savage bull approaching. Sir Dafydd proclaimed it was a demon sent from Lampeter, so he stood on Craig Ysguboriau, opened his book of spells and confronted the bull. The bull, seeing what he thought was a clergyman, pawed the ground, bent his head and charged. The conjurer stood his ground and commanded the bull to turn and follow the road back to Lampeter, which it did, goring the Lampeter conjurer to death on the way.

Sir Dafydd was making house calls in Rhaeadr and, on returning to Ceredigion, realised that he had left his book of spells behind. He sent his apprentice boy to fetch it, warning him that under no circumstances was he to look inside, but knowing with certainty that he would. The boy was a curious lad with shaggy black hair, deep eyes and an inquisitive and fearless nature. He sat down and opened the book by the banks of the Wye, the written words began to shiver and shift, and out of the book leapt a monkey demon, a big one, with furrowed eyebrows, hunched shoulders, a bald patch and long ape-like arms. It gazed around, looking gormless, and started to swear. The boy had been taught well, and despite his fear he remembered a spell, 'Tafl Gerrig o'r Afon', and immediately the simple demon leapt into the river and started throwing stones onto the bank. When there were few stones left, the boy couldn't think of another spell, so he ordered the demon to throw the stones back into the river. Then to throw them onto the bank again. This went on until the demon became angry and the idea formed in his small mind that he could either ignore the boy, or eat him. Sir Dafydd had been watching from afar, and commanded the demon back into the book, leaving the boy thinking he had just won a great battle.

One day, Sir Dafydd had been on business in Montgomeryshire, and was feeling too tired for the long journey home, so he summoned a demon in the form of a horse, a black snorting wild creature, and he rode home with his apprentice boy sat behind him, clutching on for dear life. The journey was fast and rollicking and the boy sensed that they were flying, though it was too dark to see. He had been told of another conjurer, Sir Dafydd Siôn Evan of Llanbadarn Fawr, who flew through the air on a talking demon horse, often returning after weeks away covered in seaweed or sulphur. When he got home the boy found he had dropped his sock, so in the morning he set off back along the road to look for it, and found it hanging from the topmost branch of an ash tree. The boy was convinced that Sir Dafydd had flown through the air that night.

The apprentice boy was beginning to learn a few tricks from his master, and one Sunday when Sir Dafydd was on his way to church – 'keeping up appearances' as he put it – he told the boy to be a scarecrow and keep the crows from his corn. The boy decided that chasing crows all day was too energetic, and when Sir Dafydd returned, he found the boy fast asleep under an oak tree. He was about to scold him most severely when he noticed that every crow in the neighbourhood was locked in his barn. The conjurer smiled to know his boy was learning how to command birds.

A local tailor visited the celebrated conjurer and told him that a man had come into his shop to be measured for a new cloak, but the tailor was afraid because the man wore a hood over his head, had deep eyes, big teeth, cloven hooves for feet, and smelled strongly of sulphur. Sir Dafydd advised the tailor to measure the man as agreed, but to keep behind him and never to show himself. When the man came for his new cloak, the tailor kept behind, and every time the man turned, the tailor turned too. The man commanded the tailor to appear in front of him, and there stood Sir Dafydd, who ordered the man to 'Go, and never return,' which he did, for as the conjurer had already sold his soul in return for his powers, the Devil could do little until the contract expired.

The apprentice boy was learning fast, and one day he punched the conjurer on the nose until blood dripped. Sir Dafydd stared at the boy through dark eyes, and the boy met his gaze until the conjurer threw his head back and laughed, because he knew that to draw blood from a *dyn hysbys* meant they could never command you ever again. The apprentice boy had served his time.

Sir Dafydd was the last of the colourful conjurers. Those who came after were nonetheless in demand, curing cattle, lifting curses, finding lost objects, counteracting witchcraft, laying spirits and dispensing remedies. In the 1800s Evan Morris from Goginan often consulted a conjurer when his pigs and cattle were ill. The conjurer, probably Edward Davies from nearby Ponterwyd, drew circles over a sheet of paper, filled them with indecipherable writing and symbols, and told Mr Morris to rub the paper over the animal's back from ears to tail muttering, 'In the name of the Father and of the Son and of the Holy Ghost.' This same charm worked on Mr Morris' sister-in-law's old pig. A farmer from Llangwyryfon called on Harries – either John or Henry, it's not clear which one – of Cwrt-y-cadno when his butter would not churn. The conjurer gave him a piece of paper with a spell written on it, and told him to show it to no one. On his way home, the farmer was stopped by a woman who asked to see Harries' paper. He showed it to her, and when he returned home, the spell failed to work. He paid for another spell which he showed to no one, and only then did the butter churn. The Llangurig conjurer John Morgan cured a horse of the shivers after a witch in Pontrhydfendigaid in the mid-1850s had cursed it. Around the same time, a man from Lledrod believed his belly pain was due to a woman who was terrorising the neighbourhood, and he only recovered with the help of the Llangurig conjurer. At Penpompren near Talybont a conjurer transformed a spirit into an insect, caught it in a bottle and threw it into the river beneath a bridge. In Tregaron there was a sin-eater who would place a cake or bread on the man's chest and eat it, so removing a lifetime's sins.

The Ceredigion conjurers often used the word 'abracadabra', written as an inverted triangle with one letter fewer each time until there is only an 'a' on the last line. This protected against curses, witches and the evil eye. The charms were kept in bottles on shelves in the home or near the animals.

Conjurers could be a little mischievous. Dick Spot from Llanrwst, named after a black spot near his nose, was on his way home when he was delayed by a public house at Henllan. He was charged 4*d* for a glass of beer and 6*d* for bread and cheese, which he considered outrageous, so after paying the bill he wrote a spell on a scrap of paper, hid it under the table, and left. Later that evening, the landlord saw the servant girl dancing like a mad thing round the table, shouting at the top of her voice, 'Six and four are ten, count it o'er again.' He tried to stop her but found himself joining her in her dance, both of them shouting, 'Six and four are ten, count it o'er again.' His wife, disturbed by the noise, found her husband dancing shamelessly with the pretty servant girl, tried to stop them and with a hop and a jump she too joined in the dance, all of them singing, 'Six and four are ten, count it o'er again.' A neighbour heard the racket and, guessing that Dick Spot was the cause, set off after the conjurer to ask him to release the people from his spell.

'Oh,' said Dick, 'if you wish to stop the madness, just burn the piece of paper that is under the table.' This done, the cavorting stopped and the three people collapsed to the floor, exhausted.

In the late 1950s, the librarian of the National Library of Wales received a phone call from a family in Llanidloes concerning a member of their family from Llangurig who had just died in his 90s. He was said to be the last *dyn hysbys*, who reputedly had charms and potions that could take away warts and blemishes. The librarian was asked to remove the man's papers and manuscripts, so he went to the house. The door was unlocked and he went inside. No one greeted him but he had a sense that someone was there, watching him. He went upstairs, found the papers which contained charms and conjurings, and a note that instructed him to take them to the National Library, nowhere else, not to archive or catalogue them, but to hide them in the building. Feeling uneasy, the librarian gathered the papers together and left. On returning to the library, he placed them carefully in books and manuscripts, where they remain to this day, resting in uneasy alliance with the surrounding books, as if they are alive.

Dicky Davies, farmer and conjurer from Fagwyr Fawr near Ponterwyd, was called if a dairy was afflicted, the milk yield was low or the cattle were cursed. He would open his book of spells, speak incantations and bury the milk bucket, then repeat the process with the butter clappers, and so on. The ceremony was conducted with great solemnity, and most people did not question his abilities, needing to trust in someone with powers. The conjurer would be paid for his services, often more than the family could afford, but he was considered worth it. Some children were dumbstruck by the conjurer, while others found the whole performance mumbo jumbo, and thought scrubbing the dairy from top to bottom would have worked just as well. Some laughed to hide their fear.

Once a year this conjurer caught the bus to Aberystwyth, wearing his farming clothes, and took the train to London. Before arriving at Euston he would enter the toilet, change into his dress suit, silk top hat and waistcoat, and join all the conjurers from the UK at the Annual General Meeting of the Magic Circle.

3.

TALES OF THE
TYLWYTH TEG

On the west Irish coast of Clare and Kerry, folk have the good sense to believe in the fairies. They are thought to be a race of people who lived there before the Irish did – echoes of the dead, the marginalised, scapegoats – feared a little, to be treated with respect, and their land to be preserved. Everyone has stories about 'Them'. On the west Welsh coast, few would admit to the existence of fairies – the *tylwyth teg* – other than as gossamer-winged flittery things that inhabit children's books or crystal shops. In Ireland, priests tolerated the little folk, whereas preachers in Wales saw them as a popish superstition to be eradicated.

The *tylwyth teg* were near human-sized, could be either kind or vindictive, had morals different to ours, and lived on the edges of our world. In Llanddeiniol a man witnessed nimble white fairies dancing in a ring; fairies with little horses and carriages were often seen in Cwm Mabws near Llanrhystud; they came to Cardigan Market from their hidden land in Cardigan Bay, where they were known as *Plant Rhys Ddwfn*; babies were taken by the fairies near New Quay and Newcastle Emlyn in exchange for changeling children, and a farmer was left money by the fairies in Goginan. Fairies also appeared at a wedding at Cors Caron; a midwife delivered a fairy woman of a baby at Swyddffynnon; they danced and ate bread and cheese in a bedroom in Aberystwyth; a servant at Perthrhys near Llanddeiniol witnessed two fairies dressed in white dancing around him on a moonlit night; an old man in the Vale of Aeron listened to the fairies singing for hours, and at Ponterwyd they knocked to warn the miners of impending danger. At Cwm Troed-y-Rhiw near New Quay, a father witnessed his daughter sitting in a field surrounded by small fairies dancing and turning somersaults, and once they saw him they fled, and were never seen again. David Jones from Talyfagan Farm heard them singing and saw them on his way home from the pub in the early 1900s, and Nancy Tynllain and her son watched fairies on small horses galloping round a hill at Llanarth, remarking on one wearing a red cloak, 'that fairy woman over there rides very much like meself.'

FLEET-FOOTED SGILTI

Amongst the oaks of Allt y Cefn near New Quay was a mound where the fairies danced, and on it grew an ancient gnarled oak known as the King Tree, said to be a door to the Otherworld. A woman named Grasi lived in a nearby cottage called Bwlch-y-Cefn. Grasi knew it was wise to treat the fairies well, so each night she cleaned her hearth, placed a bowl of water on the floor, and left bread and cheese and milk on her table. Every morning when she awoke, the offerings were gone, her cottage was cleaned, her spinning, weaving and sewing done, and a silver coin was left on her hob. Each night the same, though she had never seen them, and she felt she never should.

Then one evening, sitting in bed in her bonnet and shawl, red patchwork bedspread pulled up to her chin, she heard music coming from downstairs. She couldn't help herself; she went to the top of the stairs and watched. She saw a crowd of the little folk whirling in a 'corelw' to a fiddler dressed all in green, with a long thin nose, a long silky white beard and large piggy ears. He played fast. The dancers were panting for breath, shouting, 'Sgilti, slower,' but he played faster and faster until they all fell in a heap on top of each other, arms and legs in a tangle. Grasi giggled, just a little, and under her breath, but they heard her, and in the blink of a crow's eye they were gone. Grasi followed them, as fast as she could go, pulling her shawl over her nightdress, but all she saw was Sgilti the fiddler leaping from branch to branch through the oaks like a squirrel until he reached the King Tree, where he disappeared. When Grasi reached the tree there was no door to be seen.

From that day onwards, the fairies never visited her again, but at night, lying alone in her bed in the ropes of the *tylwyth teg*, she often heard the sound of a solitary fiddle, and as she looked out of her window she saw a figure leaping from branch to branch into the wood. She told everyone about fleet-footed Sgilti, and though she is now beneath the autumn leaves, her home is still there, although it is now called Cefn Garsi, so imperfect are we at remembering.

ELYR, THE HARPIST OF GLYNGOLAU

At Glyngolau in a little white cottage near New Quay lived a widow woman and her son, Elyr. The mother worked like a bee, but the boy was a loafer, a loiterer and a layabout, preferring to sit and play his father's harp, and drink sweet honey mead from the nearby brew house. If truth be told, he was a fine harper, always in demand to play for the *twmpaths*. Thrushes sat in a line on his harp and sang along to the beauty of his playing.

One morning in summer, his mother asked him to chop some wood, but as soon as she was out of sight, he threw down the axe and began to merrily play the airs his father had taught him. He felt himself drifting, and he saw a crowd of little folk who bound him with straw and carried him down the hill to the well at Tan-y-Fron. He fell into unconsciousness and when he came round he was in a strange land, surrounded by the *tylwyth teg*. A lady in red said she had heard he was an excellent harper and that he disliked hard work, so he was to be her harper in exchange for all the food and drink he could wish for. Elyr thanked her and said he would play, but then must return to his mother who would be worrying about him. The lady in red replied that he had shown precious little interest in his hard-working mother while he was with her, preferring the company of his harp, so now he must be satisfied to be her harper. Again, he politely refused, so she told him he was to remain with her till the end of time.

He was brought honey mead which was delicious on first tasting, but soon became sickly sweet, and the more he played, the more his fingers bled and the sicker he felt. There was no night in this country; no clocks, no time. He pleaded with the lady in red to return home, but was told that he had been no more than a hindrance to his mother. Elyr broke down in tears, his fingers in shreds from plucking, his teeth rotting, his body and mind broken, and he passed into a deep sleep. When he awoke he found himself crumpled in a field with his harp on top of him. He picked himself up and crawled home, feeling older and wiser, ready to help his dear mother with chopping the firewood. When he walked through the front door of the cottage he found a little old crone all shrunken, wrinkled and grey, consumed by poverty. She stared at him through bottle-bottom glasses, stood up and touched his face. As she stroked him gently, he began to turn to dust. As he crumbled into the cracks in the flagstone floor, he heard the old crone say, 'Elyr, my son, is that you? Have you come home at last?'

THE FAIRY BRIDE

There was once a lord and a lady and they lived in a great castle with their three sons. The two older boys had fine clothes and feasted well, but the youngest was filthy and smelly, dressed in hand-me-downs and liked to eat with the serving maids. One day the lord took his three sons out to the woods. He gave them each a bow and arrow and said, 'Whoever shoots furthest shall inherit my castle and lands.' The eldest drew back the bow and shot his arrow through the sky; the second son shot his arrow past the sun, but the youngest shot his out of sight. The lord spoke, 'The castle and land is yours if you can retrieve your arrow.' So the youngest brother set off through the woods, dressed in his rags with no shoes on his feet and only the crows for company. He walked and walked until he came to a great flat stone, and there, lying on top, was his arrow. He picked it up and a door appeared in the rock, and a lady emerged, with curling red hair and a gown of green. 'This arrow is yours?' she asked. He nodded. She took him by the hand and led him inside. There were fairies everywhere, but she said, 'Do not stare at them. You are mine, we will be married.' He wasn't allowed a say in the matter, it seemed, but she was so beautiful; her lips were the colour of fly agaric, and he was happy to go. The marriage was arranged and all the fairies came dressed in red coats, white breeches, white stockings and buckles on their shoes. 'Do not stare at them, it would not be wise,' she said. They were pulled to a church in a coach and four and were married; there was fiddling and dancing, and feasting and wine. Later, she led him to a bed-chamber, removed her clothes, and they made love, over and over. 'Now we will visit your family,' she said, and he was too exhausted to argue. The coach was sent for and they drove to his father's castle. His two brothers met him. They looked older, grown up, and they were not happy to see him, but they took him to their father, who also looked grey and wrinkled, with little of his life left.

'You have returned. Have you the arrow? I am about to offer the castle to your brothers.' The young man gave the arrow to his father and presented his wife. 'The castle is yours, boy.' But the two elder sons were suspicious and they went to consult the wise woman. 'Who is his bride?' they asked. The woman replied, 'She is the Queen of the Fairies. Do not stare at her, it would not be wise. Find out if she has a brother, and if so, ask to see him,' said the woman. They went back and addressed the fairy bride. 'Before you have the land, may we see your brother?'

'It would be better for you if you did not,' she replied, but the lord said, 'Bring him to me.'

'Very well, but do not stare at him, it would not be wise.'

The young man and his fairy bride returned to the rock and she blew a single blast on a horn. A short, thick-set man appeared, fierce of face and carrying an iron club. 'My father-in-law wishes to meet you,' she said. 'It would be better for him if he did not,' said her brother, but he set off on foot for the castle and stood in front of the lord. 'What do you want of me?' said the fairy brother. The lord realised that he didn't know and he was terrified at the fierceness of the little man, so just stared and stared at him. The fairy brother flew into a rage and struck him with the iron club, killing him instantly, then returned to the fairy rock. He told his sister, 'The castle is yours. Do not summon me again. Leave me in peace.' So they left the rock palace to the fairies and went to live in the castle. They live there still, and will until someone takes it from them. It has always been so.

JOHN THE PAINTER AND THE FAIRY RING

LISA PEN-SARN'S WARNING

Lisa told this story about the fairies who lived near a small farm, Y Gwndwn Mawr, close by Tregaron Bog in around 1900. A woman from Pengwndwn sent her servant boy to Swyddffynnon to fetch yeast for baking bread, saying, 'Don't you be late now, John.' She waited and waited, and after a year and a day he returned, asking, 'Was I long, mistress?' For he had been living with the fairies all that time, happy as a sandboy.

And Lisa said, 'Don't let your children out of your sight, for there are fairies out there in the river meadow in Trawscoed, I tell you.' And the mothers believed her, and called back their children if they strayed too far. In those days, there was a strong belief in the fairies who lived in the bog.

SHUI RHYS AND THE FAIRIES

Shui Rhys from Cardigan was 17, tall with black curly hair, skin of ivory, and eyes as dark as velvet that could never make contact with another's. Her father was a farmer and she looked after his cows, but this cowgirl liked to run barefoot, feel the cowpats squelch between her toes, pick flowers, chase butterflies, climb trees, tie buttercups in her locks and outstare hares.

One night Shui came home late, only to meet her mother's sharp tongue for deserting her cows. Shui said she had been with the *tylwyth teg*, small men in green coats, speaking a language too beautiful to describe, who danced around her in a ring playing tiny harps. Her mother never chided her, for she was fearful of offending the fair folk. Many's the time Shui was late home, until one night she never returned. Her mother searched the woods and the streams, and kept watch on the Teir nos-Yspridion the three nights when the fairies walked. A rumour spread that Shui was in a place of idle or sinful pleasure; Paris perhaps, London even. But the locals knew she had vanished into a fairy ring.

EINION'S BRIDGE

Einion came to live near Tregaron, where he built himself a fine mansion called Ystrad Caron. He was well loved by the community, for he played the harp for all the dances, and also because he built a bridge over the Teifi for everyone to use. For all his skills, he was a tormented soul, believing his home and his head were haunted by an evil genius. His melancholia led his wife to send him to convalesce in Fishguard, where he took a sea voyage, was captured by the French, taken on board a man o' war, and spent many years in prison before returning home looking like a tramp. He learnt his wife was about to remarry, so he offered to tune the harp for her wedding, and as he did so, he played.

> Myfi bia'm ty, a'm telyn, am tân
> My house, and my harp, and my fire are mine.

His wife recognised the tune and knew it was Einion. The locals, however, thought the story was too far-fetched, and that he had simply wandered into a fairy ring. His bridge is still known to this day as Pont Einion.

JOHN THE PAINTER

In Aberaeron around the 1860s, there lived a tall, gangly young man – a loafer, a dreamer, a bit of a painter – named John Davies. He had lost his job as a carpenter, but fancied he could paint walls and furniture as easily as canvases. He was cheerful and enthusiastic and had a high opinion of his artistic talent, for confidence is often given as compensation to those with limited ability. But John was touched with genius. He could play the flute; he could play Mozart and Min Mair; he was loved at the local *twmpaths*. Play music and you'll always have friends and food, but John was happier chasing squirrels to steal their fur for his brushes.

He was painting the vicarage at Nantcwnlle near Llangeitho, when he was sent the 9 miles to Aberaeron to buy provisions. After filling his rucksack, he set off back home with dusk approaching, making sure he had some bread in his pocket to appease the fairies should he encounter them. Instead of following the Aeron, he cut over the hill to Cilcennin to save a couple of miles. He thought to stop for a beer at the Commercial but knew the locals would ask him to play his flute, so he wound his weary way till he came to the Rhiwlas Arms, where the locals recognised him and invited him to play airs in exchange for drinks. By the time he'd played 'Ar Hyd y Nos' and 'Glan Meddwdod Mwyn' over and over, it was twilight and he was a little merry and remembering why he preferred painting. He set off, wobbling gently, and as soon as the light of the pub was behind him, the darkness hit him. It was as dark as a cow's stomach, the darkness you only find in Ceredigion, and he could barely see the road in front of him. A ghost owl flew over his head and his heart skipped a beat. A fox leapt out in front of him and met his gaze with yellow eyes before loping away, more frightened than John. He knew where he was; up on the moor road leading to Nantcwnlle. He was looking for the light of Peggi Ty-clottas to guide him; old Peggi's house was the only house on the moor. John made for the light, but found himself in a bog, and the water seeped through the eyeholes in his boots. He waded on and followed the light. It seemed to be moving in a circle and jumping occasionally. When he came close he could see the light was a fairy ring. Every bone in his body told him to turn, but his heart pulled him inside the ring, and there they were; dancing ladies, almost the size of himself, all so beautiful, wearing white dresses, whirling in a circle. One took him by the hand and he joined the *corelw*. He couldn't take his eyes off the girl who had taken his hand, and he danced as never before, forgetting that everyone laughed at his awkward gangly movements, for now he believed he was Nureyev, and he was so besotted with the fair face of his companion that he hadn't noticed the dancing had stopped.

The air was still. There was a smell of honeysuckle and bindweed. All the ladies were standing, breathing elegantly while John was perspiring and panting. And then he saw her. A dignified lady with ivy and rowan berries twined in her hair, cheeks pinched as pink as campion, a flowing gown of red. The Queen of the *tylwyth teg*. 'Who are you, mortal?' she asked. 'My name is John. I'm a painter,' he replied with a big grin. The queen laughed. 'We have no need of painters. We are art itself. We are nature. We do not grow old or decay like you. Do you have anything to offer us, mortal?' John pulled his flute from his pocket and played airs from every land, from the 'Bonny Bunch o' Roses' to 'Banks o' the Bann'. No one moved, no one smiled, and no one danced. 'Have I displeased you, ma'am? Didn't you like my playing?' The queen spoke. 'Those are not our tunes. We are Welsh fairies.' So John broke into 'Owen Alaw' and the ladies began to whirl and caper, and when he finished, he asked for a beer, and the laughter stopped. Oh, not again, thought John. The queen spoke icily. 'We are teetotal.' Well, John played music all that night and the *tylwyth teg* danced while the queen watched. She spoke. 'Mortal man, you have pleased us. Take what you wish from us.' John, quick as a jack-the-lad, took hold of the hand of the fairy lady who had been dancing with him and asked for her hand in marriage. The queen agreed, providing they return to Trichrug Hill once a year to play. John agreed, and he and his betrothed were about to taste each other's lips when – 'Is that you, John Davies? You good-for-nothing loafer.' It was old Peggi Ty-clottas from the cottage, whose light he had been looking for. She had heard the music and seen the light and the dancing, and she thought it was a corpse candle, come to tell her someone was about to die. So she took a candle, and she found John sitting beneath a tree playing his flute, with soggy feet and a heavy backpack. He looked angry. 'You've spoiled everything. Everything. I had a bargain. I nearly had a wife.'

Peggi took him by the hand and led him to her home, muttering, 'Come on, Johnny, it'll be alright.' From that day on he played for every dance and gathering, and told everyone who would listen that he was flautist to the fairies and almost took one for his wife. Most people just smiled and said, 'Poor John. Poor long-legged, gangly John.'

John was more fortunate than many folk who encounter fairy rings. Two servants from Allt Ddu between Tregaron and Bont went out to search for their master's cattle, and one failed to return. The other was suspected of murder, so he consulted a conjuror who told him to go to a certain spot in a year and a day. He found the servant dancing in a fairy ring and pulled him out; the servant thought he had only been gone a few moments. A servant girl from the Teifi banks disappeared into a fairy ring, and was also found with the help of a conjuror who told her she must not touch iron, or she would disappear forever. One day, while she was helping the farmer saddle his horse, she touched the iron bit and vanished. Nancy from Pen Gwnden near Ystrad Meurig sent her boy to fetch a bottle of balm. He returned a year and a day later, clutching a bottle of balm, having thought he'd been gone a few moments.

In County Galway in 2012, a strong Gaelic footballer of a man, 17 years of age, said that his sister had entered a fairy ring the previous year and danced with 'them'. No hint of irony, for many folk from Galway, Clare and Kerry believe in the fairies. Even in West Wales, some folk can still tell you where there is a fairy ring.

On a walk near Pontypridd with the storyteller Guto Dafis, tracing the route taken by the heir to the Pantannas estate just before he vanished into a fairy ring, we chanced upon a very different circle. In the woods was a clearing, a circle of burnt-out tree stumps, stones, empty crushed beer cans, crisp packets, condoms and small plastic bags, a tall post with the burnt remains of blue plastic nailed to the top, and a large rock with the friendly words 'Drug Camp'. There are many ways to disappear.

THE ABERYSTWYTH
HIRING FAIR

Every November, Vernon Studt's articulated lorries roll into
Aberystwyth, transforming the salty seaside town into a fair-
ground, with dodgems, carousels, freak-outs, and fold-out lorries
decorated with images of pouting ladies, jumbo elephants and
Elvis Presley. Studt's November Fair first came to Aber in 1896,
comprising Grand Venetian Gondolas, Messrs Baker's Circus, John
North's Shooting Gallery, Crecraft's Beautiful Electronic Picture
Palace, and William Haggar's Portable Theatre Company, with

its home-made cinematographs. In those early days the funfairs were part of the much older hiring fairs, when farmers came down from the hills, dressed in their Sunday best, not to buy sheep or sell home-made jams, but to buy labour. Girls and boys with faces scrubbed lined the streets from the Angel Inn to the castle, while their prospective employers strode up and down the line like royalty at a garden party. These were the job centres of their day.

On a farm not far from the salty town lived an old couple, Huw and Bet. Poverty had been their constant companion, and all they had were the three comforts of old age: fire, tea, and tobacco. There was no one to help them on the farm, for they never had a child. Huw watched over the sheep, though his sight was failing, the marrow in his bones was freezing, the dewdrops dripped from his nose and at the end of each day he soaked his aching feet in a bowl of warm water. Bet fed the chickens and milked the cows, collected the eggs and lifted the milk churns, and at the end of each day her back was broken and her veins were varicose. She knew they would not survive another winter.

One evening they were staring at the flickering fire, broken-backed and with blistered feet when old Bet said, 'Huw, my husband, we need help. Someone who can milk the cows, feed the chickens, clean the house, stoke the fire, sew our clothes and cook us fine meals.' Now, Huw had a hedgehog in his pocket. 'Dieu, no, no, we'd have to pay her.'

'Think, my husband,' said the old woman, 'if we had a serving girl, I could knit and embroider so there would be no need to buy clothes, and you could whittle wood and be the poet you've always dreamed of. We could make money from our crafts, and save our broken bodies.' Huw was already dreaming.

So the first Monday after 12 November, they set off on foot for the November Hiring Fair in Aberystwyth, he in high-crowned bowler, waistcoat, watch chain and fob, and she with bonnet, hatpin and starched apron. They took a lift in a donkey cart and arrived smelling a little of chickens. They walked along the line of jobseekers, asking questions, feeling muscles, and inspecting hair for lice. None were quite right for Huw; they were either too tall or too plump, too old or too young, too cocky or too quiet. At the end of the line, in the doorway of the Angel, was a plain, dark girl, with jet-black hair flecked with red ochre and deep green eyes that stared right into old Huw's soul. She was clutching a small iron penknife. 'Your name, cariad?' asked Bet. 'Fi enw i yw Elin,' the girl replied, and she smiled with thin red lips that lit up Bet's life as a flickering candle would a darkened cave. A coin changed hands. No more questions were needed, no paperwork, no contracts. She was hired. Starting Monday next.

Elin soon made herself indispensable. Each morning when the old couple arose, they found a fire blazing in the hearth, and bowls of salty porridge on the table. After breakfast she sent old Huw off into the hills with a packed lunch of freshly baked bread and cheese, she helped Bet patting the butter, she walked the goats, cleaned the chickens, swept the yard and dusted the house; at the end of the day bowls of hot soup were on the table. She sat Huw down by a roaring fire with a notepad, a sharpened pencil, a copy of the great bards and a clean set of long johns. She wrapped a quilt around Bet's legs and placed embroidery on her lap as if she was a queen. Then she sat at her spinning wheel, making shawls and muffs, and she told them stories. Such stories. She was the finest weaver of woollens and spinner of yarns they had ever known, and soon the old couple were the best dressed in the county, and they loved this small, plain, dark-haired, green-eyed girl who slept with a sprig of rowan on her pillow. She was the daughter they never had.

Through the winter all was just so, but when spring came, Elin took her spinning wheel outdoors to hear the birdsong and listen to the rattling water in the stream singing to the wagtails. She came back at the day's end with her arms full of beautifully woven clothes. So it went on, until Bet began to wonder how one girl could weave so much. Her nosiness was more than she could bear, and one day she followed Elin into the woods. She watched as the girl sat spinning, and soon she was surrounded by small figures, each with a tiny loom or wheel, carding and weaving so fast that old Bet's eyes could not catch up. These were the *tylwyth teg*, and Bet knew that there would be a price to pay for this. That night Elin did not return, and the following morning the fire was full of grey cinders and no food was on the table. The *tylwyth teg* have taken her; they always do, thought old Bet.

Soon it was as it always was; Huw's feet ached, Bet's back was broken, and poverty knocked on their door. One stormy night, they were lying in bed exhausted from the day's labours, Huw snoring the sleep of the dead, Bet freeing her mind from the ropes of the *tylwyth teg*, when she sensed someone in the room. Standing at the bottom of their bed was a man, tall and gaunt, with high cheekbones and sunken eyes, dressed in russets and browns. He said, 'Lady, I wish your help,' and his dark eyes told her he spoke no lies. She threw a shawl round her shoulders and followed him, and he led her along paths she had known since childhood, past hanging oaks and mossy boulders, to a strange cave unknown to her, with a great studded doorway. He took out a key, unlocked the door, stood to one side and beckoned Bet to enter.

The doorway opened into a bright bedchamber, all carved wood and chandeliers, and lying on a golden four-poster bed with red drapes was an elegant lady, in the pain of labour. The man spoke to Bet. 'My wife, the baby has turned. You know midwifery? Help her?' Bet thought little about his strange, blunt way with words and rolled up her sleeves and delivered the screaming woman of a beautiful baby girl. The man did not smile or welcome his child or kiss his wife; instead he spoke to Bet. 'Stay a month, care for my daughter and my wife. You will want for nothing for the remains of your days.' He showed her to a small chamber and brought her the baby. 'Stay here. My girl will be brought to you each morning; bathe her once a day, rub this salve all over her body and into her eyes, but do not taint your own eyes.' And his dark stare told her she could not refuse, and he would be true to his word.

Day after day, she bathed the baby and rubbed the salve into her soft skin. Almost a month passed, and while she was rubbing ointment onto rosy cheeks, her left eye itched and without thinking she touched her eye, and her world changed. Through her right eye she saw the baby; blonde, blue-eyed and rosy cheeked, yet through the left eye it was black-haired, green-eyed and grubby. Through her right eye she saw a tall elegant man with dark sunken eyes; through her left eye she saw a small squat man with a bulbous red face and a squint. Clutching the child, she ran through the door and into the great bedchamber. Through her right eye she saw an elegant woman lying in a golden four-poster with red drapes; through her left eye she saw a plain dark girl lying in a clump of dried bracken, with only a rushlight for brightness and the earthworms for company. She stared at the girl. 'Elin?' The girl looked alarmed. 'You can see me? Say nothing. Look around you.' Bet looked with her left eye and she saw small folk dressed in russets and browns, scurrying around her. 'Listen,' said Elin, 'my mother was fair folk, and it was arranged I was to marry their king. I ran, for I knew they could not hold me to the promise if I kept an iron knife with me by day, and a sprig of fresh rowan on my pillow by night. Some of them helped me with my weaving, but he found me. One night, weary from my day's labours – you never knew how weary I was – I forgot the rowan sprig. He claimed me. My husband is a strange man, an honourable man who will not tolerate duplicity. If he believes you cannot see me, he will keep his word and return you to your man and care for you.'

So Bet pretended she could not see Elin, and at the month's end the king escorted her home, and told her she would never see him again, but she would want for nothing. True to his word, the *tylwyth teg* left eggs and milk on the farmhouse doorstep each day, their house was tidied, their cattle herded. It was as if they had a hundred unseen servants. Old Huw asked no questions, happy to have his wife returned to him. Alone with her thoughts, Bet remembered the story of Pali Evans of Swyddffynnon who delivered a fairy woman of a baby, only to have dust blown into her eyes so she never saw the fairies again.

At the year's end, the old couple, healthy and happy, dressed in bowlers and shawls, took the road to Studt's New November Pleasure Fair in Aberystwyth. The fair was busy, bright and bustling, prices were high, and talk was that the fair folk were there. They were, for Bet saw a short man with a squint and a silver sword piercing fruits and sliding them into a sack. Excited, she ran up to him and said, 'How is Elin? And your baby girl, bless her?' He squinted at her, and said, 'Through which eye do you see me?' Mesmerised by his stare, she pointed to her left eye. He raised his sword and took out the eye and brushed the empty socket with a leaf of plantain to heal the wound, and all she could see was a tall elegant man vanishing into the crowd. From that day she never again saw through her left eye. But her right eye always reminded her of what her left had seen, and her memory painted pictures in her mind, of Elin and her beautiful baby, and the *tylwyth teg*.

6

THE LLWYNWERMWNT
CHANGELING

In 1895 in Clonmel, Tipperary, seamstress Bridget Cleary disappeared amidst rumours that she had run away with an aristocrat. A week later her burned body was unearthed from a shallow grave. In fact, she had fallen ill, the doctor had refused to come, and the priest had given her the last rites. Her husband Michael, her father, her uncle – the local storyteller Jack Dunne – and other members of the family had kept her confined for a week. They said they believed Bridget had been taken and her body

replaced with a fairy changeling. She had been starved, threatened, physically and verbally abused, exorcised and burned to death by her husband. Michael was convicted of manslaughter rather than murder, as the court accepted his belief that Bridget was not human. Children today still sing 'Are you a witch, are you a fairy, are you the wife of Michael Cleary?'

Changeling stories are frequently found in popular culture, from WB Yeats' *The Stolen Child* to *Gone with the Wind*, from Shakespeare to Star Trek, from *The Omen* to Maurice Sendak. There is a story from the Ceredigion border near Newcastle Emlyn, where a conjuror orders a Cenarth boy to heat a shovel by the fire until red hot and hold it by a changeling's face. In an instant the little creature takes to his heels and is never seen again from Abercuch to Aberbargod, so the story goes. The mother finds her baby unscathed. In the story the child is not referred to as a changeling, but as one of Rhys Ddwfn's children, an old colloquial name for the fairies in West Wales. And there is this story from near New Quay.

There was a woman with lips as red as rowan berries, hair as red as russet apples, and rosy cheeks. Beautiful, well, no – she was a little crooked of back. She was lost and lovelorn, wandering in the woods when she became aware of someone behind her. She turned, and there was a man. He had deep green pools for eyes, hair in black ringlets, and a smile that revealed pearly white teeth. She was a hare hypnotised by the new moon, and he kissed her on the hand and took her by the waist and laid her down on the mossy ground and, well.

When she came to, he had done as all dark handsome men you meet in the woods in fairy tales do: he had vanished. All that day she searched for him and all the following day, all that week and all the following week, and all that month until nine months passed and she gave birth to a beautiful baby boy, with eyes as green as spring, cheeks as red as roses and a smile of pearly white milk teeth. She did the only thing she could do; she transferred her love from the man who had disappeared to her beautiful baby.

The woman lived at the Llwynwermwnt farmhouse, which stood on a hill just outside New Quay on the road to Llangrannog. Her husband was a simple, stolid man who lived with his sheep and his cattle and knew each one by name, though he barely noticed that his son bore little resemblance to him. Or if he did, he said nothing.

Late one afternoon, the woman was feeding her baby. He was such a greedy little hog that her pap had run dry, so she took a jug and went outside to milk her cow. The cow was mooing agitatedly, and refused to give milk, kicking at the pail. As she returned to the cottage, she thought she saw some small figures leaving by the open door, which she was sure she had closed. She went inside and the fire was blazing; she was sure she had dampened it down. Her baby was sitting bolt upright in his carved wooden cradle, and staring at her, and his eyes were no longer the green of spring, but the colour of brown autumn. She thought little more about it. Babies change and grow. But as time passed, she became aware that her baby was looking a little older than he ought to, lined and wrinkled, his teeth were yellow, and he was grumpy, grimacing and gnashing his teeth at the neighbours, throwing toys around, refusing his milk, and spitting into the fire to hear it sizzle. Gone was the contented child she had known. She decided to consult Old Non, the wise woman.

She wrapped her baby up warm in its cradle, tucked her skirt into her boots, and set off through the Llwynwermwnt woods and over the hill until she came to the curious old Nantypele farmhouse. She climbed the worn stone steps and rattled the fox-head knocker. The old oak door creaked open and there stood an old woman, Old Non, with a thousand wrinkles around her eyes, a smile that revealed but one solitary yellow tooth, and a single grey hair in the middle of her chin. 'Cariad, dewch i mewn. Come in, sit down by the fire. Have some bara brith and a nice cup of horrible tea, and don't mind the cat and her ways. Now what can I do for you, my dear?' The woman explained, and Old Non wrinkled her eyes, pulled on the one grey hair in the middle of her chin and said 'Cariad, this may not be your babi. It may be a changeling child. We must find out.' The old woman went over to the dresser, lifted the lid from a ceramic duck, and picked up an egg. She pricked both ends and blew out the contents. 'At harvest breakfast, lay your table with seven plates and seven glasses, take this egg, fill it with beer and lay a table with bread and cheese, and say clearly – so your babi can hear – that you are making breakfast for the men who will bring in your harvest. Listen, watch, say nothing; watch the fire in your hearth, do not turn around, come and tell me what you hear and see. Go on. Off you go, now. Shoo.'

The woman took the egg and set off home. It was dark when she returned; the moon was rising and there was a smell of mischief in the air. Her cow was mooing agitatedly. She went to the door and it was ajar; she was sure she had pulled it to. She went inside. The fire was blazing; she was sure she had dampened it down. She looked at her baby, and it stared back at her with the big brown eyes of autumn and the knowledge of a thousand and a half years. Her heart filled her belly, and dark thoughts danced in her head. Better to be done with the creature, tie it in a sack and throw it into the deep pond at Nantypele Farm and drown it like a kitten. She waited until harvest time, and when it came, she set the kitchen table with seven glasses and seven plates, ensuring her baby's big brown eyes saw her every move. She took the egg and filled it with beer, and laid a table with bread and cheese.

When she broke the egg open, there was a feast for all seven of her harvest men. She stoked the fire and stared into the flames, and she heard a voice behind her ...

> I have seen an acorn before seeing an oak
> I have seen an egg before seeing a chick
> But I have not seen egg of hen
> Making feast for harvest men.

Filled with fear and confusion, the woman ran over the hill to tell Old Non what she had heard, and the old woman wrinkled her eyes and pulled on the one grey hair in the middle of her chin and said, 'Cariad, come with me, and say nothing. Do exactly as I say.'

They set off back over the hill to the Llwynwermwnt farmhouse. By the time they arrived, the cow was near hysterical, the door was wide open and the fire was blazing. The baby was sat upright in his cradle, staring with big wide autumn-brown eyes, staring straight into their souls, gnashing its teeth and sending shivers down his mother's spine. Without a moment's thought, the old woman picked up the changeling child, ignoring the screams and threats and cursing, and carried it out of the cottage, saying it must be hurled into the Nantypele pond. The woman was terrified and refused, but Old Non set off over the hill towards Nantypele, the child shrieking and biting and imploring the mother to free it from the old woman's grasp. They ran through the farmyard and down the path to the deep, dark pond. Old Non plucked the one grey hair from the middle of her chin and dropped it in the dark water. Then she took the changeling, stared into its bloodshot brown eyes, ignored its screeching and swearing, and hurled it as far as she could into the pond. As it hit the surface, the waters boiled, the baby cursed and howled, and the *tylwyth teg* appeared and dragged their wayward child into the depths, leaving a clinging coldness in the air.

The woman was near deranged, but said nothing. Old Non took her by the hand and led her back along the track to her farmhouse. The door was latched; they opened it and went in; the fire was dampened, the old woman brought it to flame with the bellows; and there in his cradle, sleeping soundly, was her own beautiful baby, with cheeks as red as roses and a mouth full of white milk teeth. All was as before; her baby had been returned, and the woman clutched him to her breast and nearly squeezed the life out of him, she was so happy. As she stared into his eyes, she noticed that while one of them was as green as the spring, the other was still as brown as the autumn.

7

THE LADY OF
FELIN~WERN MILLPOND

The Felin-Wern farmhouse stands by the mill next to the crook-backed bridge at Gilfachreda, and here there lived a miller, his wife and their son, Moses. He was a good-looking lad and he knew it: he had curly black hair, sloe-black eyes and a smile that charmed all the ladies of New Quay, who giggled and flushed when they saw him. He worked hard at the mill, oiling the great wheel and threshing the corn, and at the end of each day he would stroll by the old mill pond, enchanting the foxes and entrancing the lovelorn toads who lived in the cracks of the drystone wall.

One warm evening with the full moon shining, Moses saw a figure sat on the drystone wall on the side of the pond away from the road. It looked like a woman, but he knew all the girls around, and this was a stranger. She wore sandals; no local girls would wear sandals – they were too flirty – they wore *closhwns*, or clogs. He edged closer, his gaze not leaving her, and he shouted, 'Good evenin', lovely moon tonight.' The girl stared at the moon's reflection in the water. Moses was not used to rejection. 'Don't fall in,' he said, 'this pond is deep.' She didn't even look at him, but persistence was his middle name. 'You look like you might be lost. What's your name? Can I help you?' The girl turned and stared at him. 'Find my sandals. My name is of little importance.'

Quick as a scurrying lizard on a warm day, he was round the pond and by her side, and oh, his heart missed a beat. She was more beautiful than he could ever have imagined, with a sheaf of hair the colour of ripe corn, deep green eyes of rain-soaked grass, and a mouth like spring water. He'd fallen hopelessly in love. He scurried round, looking for her sandals, searching every bramble patch, pawing the ground like a poodle digging for a bone, blood dripping from the thorn scratches on his hands, though he felt no pain and he found nothing. She stared at him for a moment. 'Thank you. I have my sandals,' she called, and she vanished. He called for her, searched for her and cursed her, for he knew he was in a fairy tale.

Being a simple lad who was used to women falling for him, he asked his mother's advice. 'Keep away,' she said, 'she's one of the *tylwyth teg*, she's trouble. Find yourself a nice local girl, not too pretty. Pretty ones will break your heart; plain ones will bake you fairy cakes.' So every evening after work, he ignored his mother's sage advice and walked round the pond waiting for a glimpse of the girl, but all he found were lovesick toads and an elegant bachelor frog. Seven evenings passed, and another seven, until at the next full moon he saw her, silhouetted in moonlight, holding a bulrush – the wand of the fairies – and standing in the mill pond up to her knees. 'Come here,' he called, 'you'll drown.' She stared at him. 'It's the night before summer. Here I'll stay.' He kept talking: why did she disappear, where did she go, when can he see her again, what's her name, how can she be standing up to her knees in a 30ft-deep millpond? All she said was, 'My name is beneath the water, and is of little importance.'

'Then,' said Moses, 'I will call you Siriol. How do you like that? Now you have a name. And you have my heart. I think of none but you.' She just looked at him with those green eyes from beneath her mane of corn and said, 'I am not from here. I am not the same as you. You cannot own me.' But Moses was bursting, the moonlight was tugging the water in his body, churning his mind and overwhelming his heart. 'Let me come with you to your home. I will marry you, damned if I don't.' But the girl looked at him with emotionless eyes, and said it would be better if he did not. 'You will never see your family again. No sacrifice is worth that.' And she disappeared as before. Moses swore. 'No, please don't do this. I will not go away. I will be here by next full moon. I will make sacrifices.' And he barked like a fox.

Moses told his mother and she said 'Moses, you numbskull, she is a fairy. She will take you to her world and we will never see you again, or she will come here and be miserable and turn us all into toads. What about Carys from the little house with the red corrugated iron roof? She's a nice girl who can bake a tidy cake.'

Next full moon he was there, stalking the pond like a wild fox, with yellow eyes and hunched shoulders. Siriol appeared from the pond, dripping with snails and pondweed, like Ginny Greenteeth. He pleaded with her to have him; he would live in her world, anything to be with her. She stared at him. 'I shall ask my father.' As she vanished, he threw his head back and howled. Another month passed, and there he was, unshaven, sunken dark eyes, a mane of black hair, looking for all the world like Lestat or Lugosi. When he saw her he leapt at her, but she turned and faced him, rooting him to the spot, those deep green eyes staring straight into his sloe-black eyes. 'My father has spoken. You will spend six months in our world, then return here for six months. At the year end, you will know your heart.' Moses growled and slavered, pleaded and begged, promised her his heart was true; if he didn't have her, he would die. All she said was, 'The corn is sown.' She stepped out of the water and told him to stand on a small ring of grass greener than the rest. She stamped her foot three times, almost squashing a lovesick toad who was trying in vain to climb on top of his beloved's back. Moses was

surrounded by the *tylwyth teg*, and in the blink of a crow's eye he was
in a strange land, his anger departed. He felt a curious contentment;
there was no night, no clocks, no sense of passing time, and he had
no memory of a past, not even a fleeting moment – there was only a
mist. It was not happiness or love or comfort; there were no words to
describe this, no language. He spent all his time with the girl; then
her father told him that six months had passed and he was to return
to the mill and think on his daughter. He fell to a swoon and when
he awoke he was by the mill pond with no memory, only a sense of
sweet melancholia, though he remembered every emotion he had
ever felt. A toad jumped onto his chest and croaked.

He went to see his parents, who thought he had only been gone
a few moments. All he could remember was that he must return to
Siriol's home after six months. His parents were saddened at the
thought of losing him, but they could see he was speaking truly.
He spent the next six months working for his father, grinding
corn and threshing grain, with a sense of serenity he had never
known before, the wild animal inside him gone. Every night he
was serenaded by a chorus of forlorn frogs and lovesick toads.

At the next full moon she appeared and he told her without a
word passing between them that he was coming with her, but there
was sadness in his heart, because he knew he would never see his
family again. Tears were streaming down his face, dripping from a
dewdrop on the end of his nose and being caught by a small toad.
The girl leant forward and kissed him and dried his tears. 'There is
no need. I will live here with you. My father gives me a dowry of
seven white cows for your family. They will give you the finest milk,
yellow cream and crumbling cheese beyond your dreams. There is a
price, for each year on May Day eve, I will return to my family for
one day, and you will never question me about it. Never. Do you
understand?' Moses agreed and returned to his family, and there was
feasting and celebration when they heard that he was not leaving.
Siriol and Moses were wed, the herd of white cows arrived and began
flirting with the Welsh Blacks, and within a year Siriol had given
birth to a baby boy with sea green eyes, each cow had given birth to a
white calf, and there had never been so much toadspawn.

On May Day eve she disappeared and returned a day later. This went on for seven years and seven sons. And as time passed and their sons grew, Moses became wrinkled and bent of back, while she never looked a day older than when he had first met her. She worked hard and cared for her boys, she was honest and straight in her dealings, but she didn't tolerate fools. Some said she was an enchantress. She called an old man a hunchback, and he grew a hump where there had been none. They said she turned little boys into toads, and certainly the old millpond was frothing with more toads than ever before.

One day Moses, with snow-white curly hair and watery eyes, died. After the funeral, Siriol called her grown-up sons to her and told them she was returning to her own land, but that she would always be watching over them. She kissed them all goodbye, told them to beware of beautiful strangers who would bring nothing but trouble, and to look for wives who were nice plain local girls who could bake fairy cakes. And she vanished.

8

THE SALTY
WELSH SEA

In the old Welsh Dreamtime, when men were men, women were women and fish were fish, there lived three brothers in a yellow limewashed farmhouse on the old Welsh tramping road. The eldest brother ploughed the land and had honey on his bread, the middle brother ploughed the sea and had salt in his porridge, and the youngest ploughed his own furrow and had fluff in his pocket. He was an artist; a loafer; a wanderer. He walked the old Welsh tramping roads with a rucksack on his back and a tune on his lips, and when his belly grumbled, he tried to sell a painting but no one bought them, for he lacked talent, so he would cheerily call on his brothers and beg for food. Soon the righteous noses of the two hard-working brothers grew sick of the smell of him.

'Little Brother,' said the eldest. 'If I were to give you an enchanted pig, what would you give me in return?' This was a time when pigs were more valuable than gold; a war had been fought over enchanted pigs. Gwydion, the old trickster of Gwynedd, stole pigs from the court of Pryderi, King of Dyfed. Pryderi chased Gwydion back to Gwynedd, and there was a battle which ended with Pryderi's death. The boy replied, 'I would give you anything for a pig, dear brother.' Eldest Brother went out into the farmyard and returned with a small pig on a rope. 'Here is your pig, Little Brother. Now, if you will, please go to Blazes.' So little brother set off along the old Welsh tramping road with his pack on his back, a tune on his lips and a pig on a rope.

All that day they walked, boy and pig whistling and squealing in harmony, until they realised they didn't know who or what Blazes was. They came to a cottage and saw a hoary-headed man trimming a hedge in the shape of a mermaid, covering her modesty with ivy. 'Good evening, hoary-headed man. Would you, by any chance, be Blazes?'

'No, no, my boy, you have me quite wrong. I have hardly a friend in the world. But you will find Blazes in a cottage at the end of this winding way through the woods. You will recognise it for the smoke billowing from the chimney and the firelight shining through the windows. But a word in your ear, Mr Blazes and his friends are particularly partial to roast pork.' The pig's ears pricked up. 'He will offer you anything for your plump little friend, but take my advice, he has only one object worth exchanging for, and that is an enchanted handmill he keeps behind his front door. This handmill can grind out anything you wish, your heart's desires.'

Little Brother knew nothing of the perils of wishes in fairy tales, so he thanked the hoary-headed man and set off through the darkening wood, the pig reluctant to follow, tugging on the rope and squealing. In the shadows of the wood they came to a big house, with smoke tumbling from the chimneys and firelight pouring from the windows. He rattled the knocker on the great oak door. It opened immediately, and there stood a tall elegant man with a reddening face and high cheekbones, surrounded by his friends, who were poking the fire in a great hearth with their long noses. They drooled at the sight of the pig, testing its plumpness with their hands and shouting, 'Pork, pork, give us pork!'

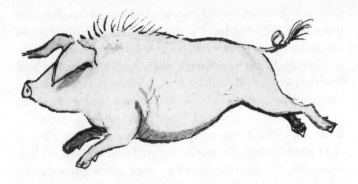

'Excuse me, but are you Mr Blazes?' The man replied instantly, 'Incarnate,' and offered Little Brother a cool thousand for the pig. The pig was relieved to hear the offer rejected. Mr Blazes offered more and more; a seat in the government, ratbane for his less popular brothers, hair restorer for the bald patch on his head ... all were turned down. 'I have no need of riches or power. I love my brothers, and it's not baldness, just the way the light falls on my crown. But there is one thing ...'

Blazes and his friends pushed their pointy faces closer to Little Brother, drooling and slavering. 'Yes, name it.'

'I would exchange my pig for an enchanted handmill.'

'No, oh, no,' said Blazes, 'no, no, no,' but the floor was now slippery with slaver, they were chanting, 'Pork, pork, give us pork,' and some of Blazes' friends were biting pieces from his bony legs and elbows, so the deal was done. The handmill was handed over, and so was the pig, squealing as the door closed, and that is where we must leave him. Maybe he was eaten, maybe he ran up the chimney, built himself a house of bricks, outwitted a wolf and lived happily ever after?

Little Brother whistled his way back along the old Welsh tramping road with the handmill beneath his arm, and no thought for the poor pig. He passed the house of the hoary-headed man, who showed him how to start the handmill by saying, 'Little mill, little mill, grind me my warmest wish,' and how to invite it to stop. Little Brother whistled his way along the old Welsh tramping road, and the hoary-headed man watched him go and shook his hoary head, as if he had seen all this before. He came to the shores of Cardigan Bay, within a pig's holler of his elder brother's house, and he thought this was where he would live. He set the handmill down and spoke, 'Little mill, little mill, grind me a handsome house, Little mill, little mill, grind it without a mouse,' and the handmill ground out a pink limewashed Welsh longhouse with a chimney at either end, a table, a chair, meat and wine for the table, until he had all he needed, simple boy that he was. And as he settled down by a roaring fire that night, he ground out some paints, brushes, and a sketchbook, and he thought to himself, 'This going to Blazes is a fine sort of thing.' Then he ground out a red bantam cock to wake him in the morning so he could start to paint early. There was no need to beg from his brothers ever again, although the handmill was quite unable to make him a better painter.

Up at the yellow limewashed farmhouse, Eldest Brother saw smoke from a chimney, so he set off to investigate. There was a pink limewashed Welsh Longhouse that hadn't been there yesterday, and he thought it must be a *tŷ unnos*, for in Ceredigion if you can build a house in one night and have smoke pouring from the chimney by the following morning, you own the land all around. He knocked on the door and his eyes were as wide as teapots to see his little brother. 'Brother, only yesterday you had not two pennies to rub together; you were as poor as a church mouse, yet now you are as wealthy as a king. Where in Blazes did you get all this wealth?'

'From behind the kitchen door,' replied Little Brother, with equal truth and wariness. Eldest Brother produced a bottle of homebrewed beer and soon they were sat under the kitchen table together, and Little Brother's tongue was loosened, and he told him all about the handmill, and then he passed out, drunk as a lord.

Eldest Brother took the handmill home to the limewashed farmhouse, placed it on the kitchen table and thought of what he desired most. Beer and women. 'Little mill, little mill, grind me maids and ale. Little mill, little mill, grind them dark and pale.' The handmill began to grind. It ground out a wave of strong beer

until it splashed over his boots, and then he added, 'Oh, and fish
for a feast.' The handmill ground out a dark naked girl, with the
tail of a fish. Then a pale one, also with a tail, and a tawny one.
And soon the beer was up to his knees, his belly, his chin,
and mermaids were frolicking in the sea of ale, and he shouted out,
'Stop, for pity's sake, stop,' but the handmill continued grinding
and soon the beer burst out of the door and a river of beer and
mermaids went foaming down into Cardigan Bay. The mermaids
took Eldest Brother by the hand and carried him to the bottom of
the briny where he stayed without a bubble rising. He died happy
and drunk, with a tipsy mermaid on either arm.

Little Brother awoke with a headache and saw that the sea was
full of beer and mermaids singing rude sea shanties. He went up
to the yellow-washed farmhouse and invited the handmill to stop,
although it continued to grind out a drop of beer and the occasional
mermaid. He walked home, thinking not about his brother, but
how nice his house would look with a golden roof, so he asked the
handmill to grind out golden tiles and soon his humble home shone
out far across the Welsh sea.

Middle Brother, the one who ploughed the sea, was returning
home in his red-masted ship laden with a cargo of salt brought
from a faraway land, and he could see the golden roof shining.
As he sailed into Cardigan Bay he could smell hops, and the sea
was full of rowdy mermaids who were impolitely inviting him
to remove his trousers. His men, starved of female company
after months at sea, leapt overboard and were never seen again.
He found the yellow limewashed farmhouse empty, so he went
to visit the pink limewashed Welsh longhouse with a golden roof,
and there stood Little Brother. 'Brother, when I left, you were as
poor as a cabin boy and now you are richer than a Vice Admiral.
Where in Blazes did all this wealth come from?'

'From behind the kitchen door,' replied Little Brother. Middle
Brother produced a bottle of smuggled Jamaican rum and soon
Little Brother's tongue was loose. He told all and fell into the
cinders, singed the hair around his bald patch and snored. Middle
Brother took the handmill back to his red-masted ship and thought

to himself, if only he had an endless supply of salt, he would no more have to voyage to faraway lands and risk shipwreck and scurvy. 'Little mill, little mill, grind me salty salt. Little mill, little mill, grind it without halt.' The handmill turned and ground out salt until it lay like snow over the deck and over his boots, and he and his men had to climb the red mast to escape the mound of salt, but the salt climbed higher. Soon, under the weight of all the salt, the ship sank to the bottom of the salty sea. And Middle Brother, too, died happily in the arms of singing scantily clad fish ladies.

Little Brother awoke with another headache, worse than the one before. He went to the seashore to drink some water for his hangover, but it was too salty. He saw the damage his wishes had caused, and decided to stick to painting, so off he set along the old Welsh tramping road with a pack full of paints and a tune on his lips. And the handmill? Well, it still lies on the seabed, churning out salt, beer and the occasional mermaid, and Mr Lewis Lewis, proprietor of bathing machines in the 1850s, not only protected the sensibilities of nervous gentlemen, but also provided a quick escape from the rollicking sea ladies. And this is why a swim in the salty Welsh sea leaves you feeling as if you have been dancing with drunken mermaids.

9

RHYSYN AND
THE MERMAID

One morning in July 1826, a farmer from Llanychaearn – south of Aberystwyth, where Morfa Bychan Holiday Park now stands – saw a naked woman washing herself in the sea. He considered her modesty, and then watched her for a further half hour. She was a young woman of 18, with short dark hair, a handsome face, her breasts blameless, and skin whiter than any person. She was standing in water from her waist upwards, but the water was too deep for her to stand in. She frequently bent over to drink, and there was 'some black thing, as if there was a tail turning up behind her'. He fetched his wife, children and servants. In all, twelve people saw her for ten more minutes before his wife approached her and followed her along the beach as she swam away.

Mermaids have long lived in the rocky coves and remote caves along the Ceredigion coast, far away from the prying eyes of humans. Llanina near New Quay is named after Ina, a Saxon king who was rescued by mermaids when his ship ran into difficulties in a storm. Another story says it was a fisherman and his daughter who rescued the king. A further tale tells of a mermaid who sat on a rock named Carreg Ina until she was caught in a net by the local fishermen, who then released her into the sea after she warned them of a gathering storm; those who listened to her were saved, the rest drowned. At the Battle of Agincourt, the soldiers from Ceredigion carried a flag with the county armorial of a mermaid sitting on a rock. Other mermaids were seen at Aberporth and the Teifi estuary, where one was caught by a fisherman named Pergrin near Cemmes, only to be released to walk the streets of the deep after promising to call his name three times at the coming of a storm. A rowing competition in Cardigan Bay is called the Mermaid Race in remembrance of this mermaid and the storm of 1879.

Long ages past, the sea in Cardigan Bay between New Quay and Llanon was still lowland, and on a poor holding named Tangeulan there lived a widow woman named Nidan and her only son, Rhysyn. They earned their living from the bounty of the sea, the boy as a fisherman, while his mother salted and dried the herrings, and mended his nets after the seals bit holes in them to steal his catch.

Rhysyn had dark curly black hair, deep dark eyes and ruddy cheeks, he could sing and rhyme and tell a tale; all the girls of New Quay loved him, as did many of their mothers, and even one lusty old grandmother. But Rhysyn's rambling days were over. In truth he had never been attracted to any of the dark local girls. He was a fisherman, and he liked the exotic, the unattainable; something a little saucy. He was engaged to Lowri, the new maid at the big house, Plas Llanina. She was from the south, with hair of spun gold, pouting lips, plump as a puffer fish, buttressed of bosom with a laugh like a fishwife. They were to be married on the next Saint's Day, Gŵyl Mabsant, and the bidder had been sent from door to door to announce the betrothal.

One evening in early autumn, when the sky above Cardigan Bay was full of primroses and violets, Rhysyn was out setting his nets, singing a song about Lowri to drown out the herring gulls who followed him everywhere. When he reached Ogof Deupen, the Double-Mouthed Cave, his eyes fell upon a mermaid. She was sitting on a rock in the mouth of the cave, brushing long tangled red seaweedy hair with a mother-of-pearl comb. The scales of her tail sparkled in the rising moon like quicksilver, and the evening sun cast shadows below her ribs. She appeared not to see him, or she was ignoring him, so he watched her. Rhysyn was enchanted, but then he was enchanted by any new exotic woman. He said, 'Beautiful lady, can I help you? I am at your service.' The mermaid turned and glanced at him. 'Teach me the song that I hear you sing while I watch you fishing. The one that tells of the girl with spun gold hair. I have heard you sing it many times. I am in love with that song.'

Well, there was nothing Rhysyn liked more than flattery, and he rowed a little closer. 'Indeed I will teach you the song, but only if you will tell me your name.' The mermaid said, 'Morwen, daughter of Nefus, King of the Deeps.' Rhysyn sang his song, and such was the beauty of his voice, and the closeness of this dark young man with black curly hair, that her pale skin flushed rose with the embarrassment of her feelings. 'Once is enough. I will be here tomorrow evening and every evening until I learn your song.' And she was gone, in the blink of an octopus' eye.

Rhysyn was not the kind of man to go falling deeply in love; the occasional flirtation had always been enough, and now he was engaged to the buxom Lowri, the only woman who truly made his juices flow. But he felt a strange attraction to this wild fish girl, so he returned the following moonrise, and many moonrises after that. It soon became clear that Morwen was entranced by him, and he loved that kind of power over a woman. One evening she declared herself to him. She asked him to be her man, to come with her to meet her father and walk the Deeps. Most Welsh fishermen would have been as lapdogs to an offer like this, but she was too intense for Rhysyn, and too skinny, and there were crabs crawling in her hair, so he politely turned her down and told her about Lowri, the maid at y Plas.

Morwen began to weep, twisting her tangled hair between her fingers, imploring him, thrashing the water with her tail, shrieking and shaking, her white skin reddening in the evening sky. Then the turbulence of rejection receded. She calmed and spoke. 'You will regret your decision. My father will avenge this insult.' And she was gone, in the blink of a lobster's eye.

Rhysyn went home, shaken and confused, and counted the days to his wedding. He refused to go out fishing and became cold and withdrawn. His mother, Nidan, noticed the change in her son. She called Lowri, and he was distant and silent with her, too. And Lowri thought, no, not again. Men always pulled her to them, then pushed her away. On the evening before the wedding at Llanon Church, he walked down to the shore to repair his nets, and there she was. Morwen, her head and shoulders above the water, looking calm and cold. She spoke to him. 'Rhysyn, son of Nidan, if tomorrow you go to Llanon Church, my father will take your land of Ceredigion for his own, from the Rush Fields of Llanon to the door of your mother's house at Tangeulan to the Double-Mouthed Cave. Hear my words, you and your bride will be drowned.' And she slipped beneath the waves.

The following day dawned bright and clear, and Rhysyn had to be led to the church by his mother Nidan. As they entered the church, the skies turned grey and forbidding, and he saw Lowri looking so desirable in her white dress, and he knew that she would be the only woman he would ever love. At the moment their eyes met a great storm blew the waters of Cardigan Bay over the Rush Fields of Llanon, and the house at Tangeulan, into the cave of the Double Mouth and through the doors of the church. Rhysyn was.swept out to sea on a great wave, and a woman with tangled red hair took him in her arms, and as she dragged him beneath the sea, he felt his lungs fill with water, his legs became a tail, and he swam like a fish.

All in the church were drowned that day, along with many of the coastal dwellers of Cardigan Bay, their horses and dogs, sheep and pigs. Dolphins swam where people once walked. And now, on a clear quiet day, just beyond Carreg Ina, listen and you can hear the sound of church bells ringing from beneath the waves, announcing the marriage of Rhysyn and Morwen as they walk forever in the land of the Deeps. And when the wind howls and rattles the window latches, listen to the screams of Lowri and the cries of the drowning wedding guests.

10

THE PETRIFIED FOREST

Off the beach at Ynyslas, revealed only at the lowest of spring and autumnal tides, are the petrified stumps of trees up to 4,000 years old, a reminder that Cardigan Bay was once land. This submerged world has given rise to two of the most universal stories of all: Cantre'r Gwaelod, the Lowland Hundred, the Welsh Atlantis, a land lost in a great flood, with its echoes of global warming appealing to environmentalists and film-makers alike; and Plant Rhys Ddwfn, the children of Rhys the Deep, the Welsh Shangri-La, an idyllic fabled land hidden from human eyes, appealing to the spirit and hopes of those who believe there is a better way of life, if only we could see it. Interestingly, these two stories refer to exactly the same spot, just off the coast of Ceredigion.

CANTRE'R GWAELOD

There was once a world now submerged by the sea, a land that joined the mountains of Wales to the hills of Ireland. The land was ruled over by a king, Gwyddno Garanhir, or Longshanks as he liked to call himself, and he named his Kingdom Maes Gwyddno. It was rich and fertile, low-lying, with sixteen cities and a castle, and to keep the sea at bay he ordered his finest surveyors and masons to build a system of dykes and drains, sea walls, wells and sluice gates. The honour of being Keeper of the Wells he gave to his daughter, Mererid, who defended against the sea as her father would defend against invading armies.

Longshanks loved to throw great feasts in honour of himself and his friend, Seithennin, king of the neighbouring land, a mighty warrior who had fought many battles, and a mighty drinker who had drained many a glass. They passed the nights with sweet honey wine and a boar's head, recounting past glories and confiding in drunken friendship. Seithennin cast his roving eye on the king's daughter and paid court to her, begging her to cement the relationship between himself and her father. Mererid spurned him, for she had little time for men, preferring to sleep the stormy nights alongside her sluices and pumps. She gave herself to the smooth running of the sea defences, and would not let her guard down. But Seithennin refused to take no for an answer; each time he visited Longshanks he would sweet talk Mererid, distracting her from the work she loved. All he ever received in return was a lecture on the mechanics of sluice gates, the joys of mathematics and the history of dykes. To her, he stank of drink.

One day, word reached the ears of Longshanks that invading kings were planning to lay siege to his land, to plunder his great cities for their riches. Mererid heard the rumours and, if she was honest, she wished to be freed of her father and his friend, and hoped the invading kings might leave her to run the sea defences efficiently and tidily without interference. But Longshanks and Seithennin mobilised their armies, much blood was spilt, and the crows and kites feasted. Longshanks and

Seithennin won a great victory, and exhilarated by the fight, they celebrated. They commissioned their poets to praise them, they feasted on swans, ducks, quails, geese, pigs; no animal was safe from their eyes, and neither was Mererid. Seithennin, drunk on wine and blood, would not accept her rejection, and despite her protestations that at any moment the west wind may blow and the seas rise, he dragged her from her post, and down to the Great Hall. He plied her with drink and flattery, took her by the waist, laid her down on the ground, and she was not used to the drink and her head was spinning. As a storm swirled inside Mererid, so too a great storm gathered out to sea. The skies darkened and the west wind blew and the sea found that the sluice gates were unattended. Mererid screamed as her defences were penetrated, and the land screamed as the sea walls of Maes Gwyddno were breached. The storm brought a great flood and few survived; only Longshanks, a poet named Taliesin, and a handful besides. The land that Longshanks thought he owned was taken from him, just as he had taken the land from others in battle.

In time the land beneath the sea became known as Cantre'r Gwaelod, the Lowland Hundred, and if you listen on peaceful days when there are no storms in the air or in your heart, you can hear the church bells ringing. In 2012 Ceredigion was flooded once more, with people in Llanbadarn Fawr evacuated from their homes for over half a year, giving rise to a charity event called Floodstock. In 2011 the Carnival at Borth which overlooks Cantre'r Gwaelod celebrated with a ceremony involving folk dressed as druids addressing the sunken city. They decorated floats with images of Capel Celyn, the village flooded to create Tryweryn Reservoir in the 1960s in order to bring drinking water to Liverpool. Cerys Matthews has rewritten the story for children, and conceptual artist and stand-up comedian Bedwyr Williams exhibited a piece called Cantre'r Gwaelod, an old slide projector at the bottom of a fish tank, neatly commenting on the way we nostalgically reinterpret the past. All done with a sense of irony and comedy, as befits our times.

PLANT RHYS DDWFN

Often we fail to see what is right in front of our noses. In the centre of Cardigan Bay, from the village of Aberdaron on Llŷn in the north to Cemmes in Pembroke in the south, lies another land, shrouded in the mist of our own eyes. Its founder was Rhys Ddwfn, or Rhys the Deep. His people were fair and handsome, though small; they respected their ancestors and each other, cared for the land as if it was their own, treated the animals they shared it with as their equals, and the trees and plants grew like jewels. One particular herb thrived and shrouded their land from the inquisitive eyes of others. Only if you stood on the one small clump of this herb that grew near Cemmes would you be able to see Rhys Ddwfn's mystical world, and if you stepped from the turf you would forget you had ever seen it.

But the Rhysians were growing in number; they had built more towns, and there was barely enough land to grow food to feed themselves. So they had taken to crafts, quilting, carving dolls and love spoons, forging cast iron pots, making benches and stools. They traded by sea all across the world like the Phoenicians, and they visited the market in Cardigan, where they exchanged their goods for corn. As soon as 'they' were seen at the market, prices went up and all the corn had gone by lunchtime. The poor folk said that they were the friends of Siôn Phil Hywel the farmer, but no friends of Dafydd the labourer, but at least they were honest and kept their word.

They liked to trade with a man by name of Gruffydd ap Einion, as his corn was always ripe and fresh, and they enjoyed conversation with him. He was a free thinker, a libertarian in the old fashioned way, and he was intrigued by the stories of their idyllic life. They honoured Gruffydd by taking him to the patch of herbs so he could see their land, and in that moment he saw all the knowledge in the world. Their land seemed rich beyond the dreams of men, although they had little concept of currency, only barter. Gruffydd asked how they kept themselves safe, and they told him the herbs kept them from prying eyes. There was no crime, for Rhys had rid their world of those who lived only for personal gain in the same way St Patrick had ejected snakes from Ireland. They had perfect unity, honoured each other, lived with their partners and were faithful, and cared for their children and their elderly. The only image they had was a curious drawing that Rhys had left them, which showed a creature with horns, a nest of snakes for a bosom and the legs of an ass, holding a great knife, with bodies lying all around. The image was so horrific that no one had ever wished to see that creature.

When Gruffydd stepped off the patch of herbs, he remembered his friends and their land but could never recall where the patch of herbs was. The Rhysians traded with him all their lives, but one day they came to Cardigan to be told that Gruffydd had died, and all the traders had put up their prices. They walked away and never returned. Some said they went to Fishguard instead, others said Haverfordwest, and some said Mynydd Rhiw on Llŷn. No one saw them again, although Pembroke sailors told of the green fields of enchantment they could see when approaching Wales, but if they ever tried to pull ashore, the vision would disappear from view. Watchers from the shores of Ceredigion often see the fairy islands through the mists on the horizon. The spit at Wallog, Sarn Cynfellyn, is said to be the causeway to their land. Along the west coast of Wales, the fairies are still occasionally referred to as Plant Rhys Ddwfn.

NODON'S WELL

A giant named Nodon lived on the fertile plain that is now Cardigan Bay, and he owned all the land around. Nodon was a bully, and he ordered his servant girl, Merid, to protect his well from thieves who wanted his sweet fresh water. He placed a great slate slab on top of the well, which Merid was to slide aside whenever he needed a drink or a bath. If she failed him, he promised to cut out her eyes.

A gentleman rode up to the well and asked for water for himself and his horse. Merid refused, but the gentleman was handsome and dark and he offered her wine from his horn, and she looked into his deep sparkling eyes and she thought a little sip could do no harm, and soon she was telling him about Nodon's cruelty, and the man was so sympathetic that she slid the slate to one side and gave him water. He gave her more wine and soon she was as drunk as a kipper and he took her maidenhead and rode away, leaving her in the throes of ecstasy. The well was open, and soon the waters overflowed, the land flooded, the crops were destroyed, and many were drowned. Merid was washed into the sea where she became a seagull, and she had a baby and her babies had babies and they lived in their thousands on Craig yr Adar, the Bird's Rock.

THE TALE
OF TALIESIN

At Llyn Tegid in Snowdonia lived a wise woman, Ceridwen, who had gifted her giant husband Tegid Foel with enchanted armour so his flesh could never be cut. Ceridwen had powers; she was a woman of two worlds, a dark enchantress and a crooked-backed herbalist. They had two children: Creirfyw, with her mother's ebony skin, long black ringlets, and a voice that could charm nightingales. Then there was Morfran, the most ill-tempered creature known to man or beast, with his mother's dark soul, eyes so black that the crows thought him their brother, though even the crows left him alone with his torment. He lived in the room at the top of the castle. They kept the door locked, just in case.

Ceridwen watched Morfran as he sat, breathing deeply, dark eyes staring, barely moving, except to snatch a fly out of the air with those huge hands. How could a woman so otherworldly produce a grotesque like this? She thought of drowning him in a sack like an unwanted kitten, but her own damaged soul felt for him. Even a crow thinks its offspring beautiful. She decided to gift him. He may always lack eloquence, but she could offer him prophecy and inspiration. With those he would be a wise man. She would conjure him a potion. She gathered herbs, mushrooms, bark, leaves, fungi, slime moulds, dried limbs from decaying animals, breath and odours, clippings and hair, all picked by the light of the waning moon, using carefully crafted instruments, powders and tinctures that made the skin flake. She built a great fire from peat, and boiled the ingredients in a pitch black iron cauldron conjured from her own mind. The potion had to simmer for a year and a day, so she employed an old blind beggar named Mordda to sit and stir it, for he would never see what was in front of his eyes. She found a servant boy, a guttersnipe named Gwion, a boy without a single thought in his head, to pump the bellows that kept the fire alight and the cauldron boiling.

A year passed and Ceridwen fetched Morfran from his loft. He stared at the cauldron, moving only once to eat a fat black beetle. As the moon rose, Gwion pumped with the bellows. There was a flame and a crack and the fire spat. Alarmed, Gwion stood up in front of Morfran and three drops of the potion sizzled onto the back of his hand. It burned, so he licked his hand, swallowing the drops. Gwion was confused; there were thoughts in his mind. He had never had thoughts before. He was having ideas, he felt inspired, believed he was capable of anything. He knew what would happen next. He could foretell the future.

Ceridwen roared with fury as the rest of the potion soured and turned to poison. Gwion ran, his mind now swirling with inspiration and prophecy, turning into a hare, the fastest animal he could think of.

Bide, laddie, bide, there's nowhere you can hide.

Ceridwen screamed and followed as a greyhound, and soon she was hunting down the hare. They turned and twisted and just as her tongue touched the hare's back leg, Gwion shifted into a salmon, and dived into the nearest river.

Bide, laddie, bide, there's nowhere you can hide.

Ceridwen shrieked and followed as an otter and soon she was hunting the fish down. They slipped and slithered, and just as her sharp teeth were about to bite into the salmon's flesh, Gwion became a bird.

Bide, laddie, bide, there's nowhere you can hide.

Ceridwen squawked and followed as a hawk, and they flew swerving and swirling, and just as Gwion felt her claws in his back, he dived into the barn, changed to a grain of wheat and hid himself in the grain store. Ceridwen became a jet-black hen with a red comb and darting eyes; she spotted the grain that was Gwion, and swallowed him whole.

Ceridwen's belly grew, and nine months to the day she broke water, shrieked and gave birth to a baby boy. The child had a noble brow and bright eyes, but she knew it was Gwion, and she thought of drowning him in a sack like an unwanted kitten, but he looked so wise, inspired, prophetic, and she saw who Morfran may have been. She wrapped him in a leather bag, tied a knot, placed the bag inside a coracle, covered it with skins and set it free on the water. She watched as it drifted away on the tide. Gulls pecked at it, gannets dived around it and fulmars spat at it, until one day it washed up the shore south of the Dyfi estuary.

Elffyn, son of Gwyddno Garanhir, was fishing by a weir when he saw the bag, waded into the waters and pulled it ashore, hoping it might contain gold. To his disappointment, he pulled out a baby, but the baby sang a poem to him, prophesying that he would be worth more than gold. Elffyn went to see his father. 'What have you caught?' his father asked. Elffyn replied, 'A bard.'

His father laughed, 'And what is the use of a bard?' The baby recited a poem so inspiring that Gwyddno was dumbstruck. In honour of the baby's high shining forehead and inspiring words, Elffyn named him Taliesin.

Taliesin lived with Elffyn's family in a cottage by the Dyfi, and when the boy was 14 they were invited to visit his uncle, Maelgwyn of Gwynedd. Elffyn listened to the court poets praising Maelgwyn, how beautiful and faithful his wife was, how he had the finest bards and the fastest horse in all the land. Elffyn's stomach churned. The mad wine spoke. His wife was far more beautiful and faithful than Maelgwyn's, he had the best bard and the fastest horse in the whole wide world. Maelgwyn was outraged, threw Elffyn in chains and sent his darkly handsome son Rhun to test the faithfulness of Elffyn's wife.

Taliesin knew Rhun's intentions. He transformed Elffyn's elegant wife into the red-headed serving maid, and the serving maid into the lady. Rhun set to wooing what he thought was Elffyn's wife, plied her with wine and flattery, and soon he had her in bed. He cut off her ring finger and took it back to his father, who showed it to Elffyn as proof of his wife's unfaithfulness. Elffyn laughed and said the finger was not his wife's. It was too bony, the nails were too long and there were traces of rye bread beneath them. Maelgwyn grumbled, threw Elffyn back in chains, and challenged him to produce a bard better than his court poets. Taliesin was sent for.

As Taliesin walked past each of the court poets, he stared them in the eye, placed his finger to his lips and played 'blabber blabber' with them. As they were called upon to praise Maelgwyn, all that came from their mouths was 'blabber blabber'. The court poet laureate, Heini Fardd, was called for, and he blabbered more than any of his minions. Maelgwyn demanded an explanation. Heini explained that a boy had enchanted them. Taliesin was called for and he introduced himself as Elffyn's bard. Such was the strength of his rhyming that he summoned up a whirlwind that blew through the hall, sang a poem that melted the air and shattered the shackles that bound Elffyn, and Taliesin announced that he had won the contest of the bards. Maelgwyn was furious, and challenged them to a horse race between two dozen of his finest stallions and Elffyn's pony. Taliesin took bets, enchanted the pony, it won and Elffyn had all the wealth that he had hoped to find in the leather bag, and Taliesin's prophecy came true. However, for all his gifts, Taliesin failed to see the tongue lashing and bottom kicking that Maelgwyn and Rhun were about to receive from a furious red-headed serving maid who wanted her finger back.

TALIESIN'S BIRTH

Einion, a shepherd, is lost in a mountain mist, and finds himself in a fairy ring. A little old man appears, takes him by the hand, leads him to an oval stone and taps on it with his stick. The stone rolls aside, the little man places his finger to his lips, and leads Einion along a path to the Otherworld. They arrive at a mansion, climb the steps and step inside. The high hall is full of gold but there is no one to see it; there are musical instruments hanging on every wall, but no one to play them; there are tables laid with a feast but no one to eat it. Einion fills his belly, and his plate vanishes.

The little man has three daughters, and Einion wishes with all his heart to speak to them, but he has no words. His tongue feels like a lump of ice in his throat. One of them kisses him on the lips; he is enchanted, words pour from his mouth like silver coins, and the more she kisses him, the more eloquently he speaks. Soon he is using words he has never heard of, and the more he talks, the more charmed he becomes.

Einion is homesick, so the little man says he can take as much gold as he wishes providing he returns within a year and a day. He fills his pockets and is gone. At home no one recognises him, for they remembered a simple shepherd boy and now they see a silver tongued charmer with gold in every pocket. He is a stranger in his own home, so at the end of a year and a day he returns to his enchantress. They are wed without fanfare, but he is a stranger in this land, too. He is between worlds: liminal, marginal, a man of no man's land. He leaves with his wife on two snow-white ponies and they live on the shoulder of a misty mountain, where they have a son, and they name him Taliesin, the enchanted child of an otherworldly mother and a man from nowhere.

On the hillside above the village of Tre Taliesin on the Dyfi
Estuary is a large rock named Bedd Taliesin, said to be his grave.
There had once been a grander site nearby composed of standing
stones and circles, which local farmers used for gateposts, much to
the anger of visiting antiquarians. If you lie on the grave, you will
awake either mad or a poet. A current troubadour from Tre Taliesin
lay on the grave and asked the pertinent question, 'What happens
if you're a poet already?'

THE OLD TOAD OF BORTH BOG

The old, old Eagle of Gwernabwy was wrinkled with age and so very wise. He was a gloweringly gloomy old soul, prostrate with dismal, much like a miserable old poet or a lowering preacher; little wonder he lived all alone. His wife had long left him, tired of his pontificating and prevaricating. His children owned all the woods and waters around, and all he had left was a small stone on top of a mountain. He had many stories to tell but no one to tell them to; such wisdom to pass on, but no one to listen; so much love to give and no one to receive it. 'I would be so much happier if only I had a companion,' he thought. 'I shall have to find myself another wife.'

So he began to think about a bird who would make a suitable companion. He was so wise that he knew a young wife would only make him sad, for he would never be able to satisfy her needs, she would always be looking around at younger chicks, and a pretty bird wouldn't want an old coot like him, anyway. No, he needed someone as old and dull as he, so they could sit on a branch all day long and discourse interminably on philosophy and politics. He took out his little book of birds and made his way down the list. Nightingale, no, too sweet. Cuckoo, a philanderer. Magpie, a rogue and a thief.

Then he found her. The Owl of Cwmcawlwyd. Owls must be every bit as old as eagles, but how could he be sure? It would be rude to ask her age. She probably wouldn't tell him, and she might peck him. So he decided to ask the advice of his friends.

He went to see the Stag of Rhedynfre, who was dozing beneath a great withered oak stump. 'Good morning, Stag.' The stag choked on his grass. 'Bother, I thought this stump would hide me. What do you want?'

'Well, I've decided to get married but I have no one to marry except Owl. But I need to be sure she is old, and I thought you might know her age?'

The stag shook his head and snorted until the velvet fell from his antlers. 'I am so old I knew this withered old, old oak stump when it was an acorn. An oak is 300 years in growing, 300 years in its prime, 300 years in dying, and 300 years withering. Owl was old when this tree was an acorn. But don't take my word; there is one who is older than myself. Ask the Salmon of Llyn Llyw.' And the stag closed his weary eyes and pretended to sleep.

Eagle thanked Stag and went to the river to find the salmon, who was sheltering beneath the bank. 'Good Morning, Salmon.'

'Bother, I thought my camouflage would hide me. What do you want?'

'I've decided to marry Owl, but she doesn't know yet, and I must find out how old she is. Stag thought you might know.'

'I am as old as the number of scales on my body, added to the spots on my belly, added to every grain of spawn I have ever produced. When I was a fry, Owl was already very old.

But there is one who is older than myself. Ask the Ousel of Cilgwri.' And the salmon began to gently gibber.

So Eagle thanked Salmon and found the ousel sat on a small stone. 'Good morning, Ousel.'

'Bother, I thought my white breast would hide me in the dappled sunlight. Yes?'

'I'm marrying Owl, but she must be old and wrinkly and interested in talking about maladies. Salmon thought you might know her age.'

'You see this stone I'm sat upon? I'm so old that I remember when this stone was so big that 300 oxen couldn't pull it. Every day I have sharpened my beak on it until it was reduced to this small boulder. You can imagine how long that has taken. When I was a fledgling, I only remember the owl as being very, very old. However, I may be older than Stag and Salmon, but there is one much older. Go to the county of Ceredigion, take the path to the bedevilled bog of Borth, and there you will find an ancient toad. If he does not know the answer, then there is not one who does.' And the ousel fell off the stone and lay on her back with her legs waving in the air.

Eagle thanked Ousel and set off following the old Welsh tramping road towards the west. He found the toad, sitting on a stone in the middle of the bog, blinking his orange eyes at the bright Ceredigion sunshine, puffing his chin in and out, looking for all the world like the back of an old man's hand, leathery, wrinkled, warty and spotted with brown blotches. He thought to himself, this Borth is a queer sort of place.

'Good Afternoon, Toad, sir,' said Eagle. 'I have been sent by Ousel, Salmon and Stag.' The toad blinked. 'You see, Owl has consented to be my wife, and I can only marry her if she is a geriatric wrinkled old crone. So I must know how old she is, but I can't ask her or she might bite me – you know how it is, you're a toad of the world. So how old is she?'

The toad sat there. Breathing and blinking, blinking and breathing. An hour went by, and not a word. He had the look of an amphibian with advanced senility, his mind flitting in and out of sanity, speaking only when he thought he had something to say. Finally, he croaked, 'She's an old hag, that owl. I only eat dust, you know'.

'I beg your pardon, sir? Does that have any relevance?'

Half an hour went by, more breathing and blinking. 'And I never eat half enough dust to satisfy me. Do you see those hills?' Eagle said nothing. It was like being in a retirement home for terminal toads.

'I am so old, so very old, that I remember when the earth was completely flat. Flat as a pancake it was, and as high as the highest mountain. I have eaten all the dust that filled the valleys. All the land between the hills all around the world. Yet I only eat one grain of dust a day. I am careful as I don't want to eat all the dust before I die; that would not be sensible or sustainable. I am so old I don't even remember being young. I don't even know if I ever was young. Though I do remember a night in a drainage ditch with a pretty natterjack. Oh my, now where was I? Yes, I remember, I am old, but Owl is older than me. Marry her, you dimwit. She's an ancient wrinkled harridan, she'll keep you awake at night with her endless too-whitting, she'll drive you nuts with her pointless philosophising, but you'll marry her because you're a numbskull.'

The eagle should have been annoyed with the toad's telling of the truth, but he was happy to forgive because the toad had given the correct answer. The owl was old enough to be his wife. 'Thank you, dear Toad, thank you a thousand times.'

'Halfwit,' croaked the toad.

So the eagle proposed to the owl, who couldn't believe her luck and accepted without delay. She'd been on the shelf far too long and had given up all hope. She loved having someone who would listen to her endless prattling. She never used a couple of words when a couple of thousand would easily do. She talked all through the wedding service, forgetting to say, 'I do,' and not even remembering to thank Stag, Salmon and Ousel, who were chuckling to themselves. She carried on talking as they set off for their honeymoon, but to tell the truth, Eagle was so happy. For the first time in his life he could sit back and listen and be fed on fresh mice that she caught for him. It was better than any turgid poetry reading.

And Toad? Well, he'd been invited to the wedding, but had forgotten all about it. He was thinking about his night with a pretty natterjack in a drainage ditch, knowing that his imperfect memory was quite delightful.

THE OLD HAG OF BORTH BOG

One day, a girl from Tre Taliesin told the headmaster of her school in Talybont that she would not be coming in the following day. The headmaster was outraged that his pupil dared to choose to take a day off her lessons, so asked her why. She replied, 'Please sir, I shall be shaking tomorrow.'

The folk of the parish of Llangynfelyn, particularly the villages of Borth and Tre Taliesin, had been troubled for generations by the shaking. It was a fever, and the symptoms were particularly bad in the weak and old. At first they felt sickly, then their whole body started shaking – often so violently their beds rattled – and they would be unable to speak. This went on for as long as an hour once a day, but one hour later each day, for eight to ten days, until their strength slowly returned and the shaking stopped. Doctors were rarely consulted, because they didn't know what the illness was or how to cure it, and the locals were too poor to travel to the surgeries in Aberystwyth or Machynlleth. Some said it was the hatters who lived in Llangynfelyn who used mercury in the felting

process that drove them mad. Others called the illness *y hen wrach*, the old hag, after the old woman who lived on Borth Bog, the vast raised mire that separated the two villages.

The old hag came out on misty nights, opened windows, entered houses and breathed into people's faces. They woke the next morning from a restless sleep full of bad spirits, feeling depressed, and later that day the shaking would begin. The residents of Llangynfelyn believed the hag only left her home in the bog in the dead of night or in thick fog because she was ashamed of her ugliness. Teachers told the children to keep their windows closed at night and they would be safe. The locals believed the only cure was to cease burning peat from the bog, so as not to disturb the hag.

Betsen lived at Llain Fanadl, on the edge of the bog. One evening she was walking home after cutting peat, when through the mist she saw a woman sitting on a hummock of sedge. The woman had a large head, jet black hair that fell in a huge wave down her back and coiled up on the floor, and she was eating buckbeans and frog meat. Betsen called, 'Good evening.' The woman turned and stared at her with yellow eyes, then rose up like a serpent, 7ft high, thin, bony and yellow-skinned, with teeth blacker than her hair, hissed in Betsen's face, then disappeared. Betsen was in shock, but found her way home where she was calmed by her sister. After two days she was wracked with pain, fell into a fever with hallucinations and nightmarish visions, appeared to be recovering but then died an agonising death.

In the early 1900s the disease vanished. The bog was being reclaimed and drained, and the villagers were burning coal instead of cutting peat, so the hag was disturbed no more. The scientists said that the insects that carried malaria were dying out with the decrease in the size of the bog. The locals said that the hag died during a particularly freezing winter. When he was a boy in the 1960s, storyteller Anthony Morris from Borth found her home beneath an old manhole cover shaped like a pagoda, and shouted down it three times, 'Die, witch of the bog.' The hag chased him and his friends towards Tre Taliesin, and as they reached the safety of dry land, he turned and shouted, 'Die hag, die,' and she has never been seen since.

The bog is now a UNESCO Biosphere Reserve, home to otters, red kites, the small red damselfly, the rosy marsh moth, the bog bush-cricket, and three species of carnivorous sundews that eat the rare insects. But the rarest creature of all, the old hag, may now be extinct.

DAFYDD MEURIG AND THE DANCING BEAR

Dafydd Meurig of Bettws Bledrws was a lazy boy who thought he was a poet. His father rose early in the morning, made salty porridge for breakfast, and kept watch on his sheep until the frost whitened his beard. Dafydd stayed in bed, wrapped up warm in his great quilt, scribbling down important thoughts and waiting for his porridge to be brought to him. One morning his father said, 'No porridge for you, my boy, not till you help your old father with the sheep.' Dafydd was angry. 'You love those sheep more than you love me. If you don't give me my porridge, I'll leave home and make my fortune.' His father said, 'Porridge and poetry!

There's the door, my boy,' and he went back to his sheep. When he returned, Dafydd had vanished.

Dafydd tramped along the old drovers' road through the Long Wood to Lampeter, the wind in his hair, pack on his back and a tune on his lips. He had struck a deal with a drover who paid him to drive cattle to London, where he would sign on board a tramp steamer and see the world. He was weary from walking when he reached Craig-y-Ddinas and saw an old hazel tree, a thousand and a half years old. He cut himself a staff, just long enough to help him on his way, and in the blink of a crow's eye he was on London Bridge. He saw a man, a magician, a wizard, but not one with a long grey beard, a pointy hat and a cloak with moons and stars: no, you only see those in films. This was a real one, a conjurer, a *dyn hysbys*, a farmer from the Welsh hills, who had left his sheepdog, quad bike and book of spells behind, and caught the train to Euston for the Annual General Meeting of the Magic Circle. He was dressed in his Sunday best bowler, a close-cut grey beard with bits of leftover food in case he got hungry on the journey, a waistcoat over layers of grey and brown cardigans, and flip flops, and socks, one grey, one brown, with holes. 'Ah, my little puffin. I've been expecting you. What kept you? What do you seek? Magic? Morgana? Amour? Myrddin? Me? And where did you find that hazel stick? No, don't tell me, I'm a conjurer, you know. Return to that old hazel tree, and you will find riches beyond your wildest dreams, not money, you understand, something far more valuable, my little guillemot.' And he vanished.

Dafydd spent a night in London, guttersnipes pulling on his coat tails and picking his pockets, watching the lights of the Thames barges and the mudlarks salvaging scrap washed up on the riverbanks, sampling the delights of the burlesque cabarets of Soho. In the morning the conjurer was waiting for him, and they set off tramping back along the old drovers' road. They reached Craig-y-Ddinas and there was the tree, exactly as Dafydd remembered it. Where he cut his stick there were earthen steps leading down, and he found himself at the mouth of a cave, ferns and mosses hanging from the ceiling, brambles and thorns tugging at his trousers and small furry things nibbling at his toes. Dafydd stepped inside and blinked. The cave was dark and dank, but there were holes in the roof and shafts of light shining down like sword blades. It echoed to the sound of snoring and shuffling. He could see rows of sleeping men, slumped around a great oak table, higher than a flea's jump from the floor, covered in animal skins like hibernating bears. All had long grey beards, stretching to the ground so the fleas could hop on board and feast. They looked more like Rip Van Winkles than Sleeping Beauties, as if they had been sleeping there for a thousand and a half years. They had. Dafydd knew this story. He knew he was in a fairy tale. These were Owen Lawgoch's men, waiting for the call of their country, to save their people from the ravages of injustice, inequality, and incarceration. Had he been sent here to wake them? Was this the wealth the old Myrddyn mentioned?

How could they live all these years, asleep without food or water, wine or meat? As if to answer his question, a crow flew in through one of the holes, perched on the chest of a sleeping man, and dropped a worm in his mouth as it would feed one of its chicks. The man licked his lips. A jackdaw, the comical crow, flew in and dribbled a drop of water from its beak down another man's throat. A magpie, the criminal crow, flew in and tucked a peg doll under a man's arm. Dafydd looked round; all of them had dolls tucked beneath their arms.

What the story books hadn't told him about was the smell. The stench of a thousand and a half years of men not showering, a thousand and a half years of men with rotting teeth and no tooth-paste, a thousand and a half years of grown men farting in their sleep and no air freshener. He retched, and stumbled back into a table, knocking the sword from the hand of a man asleep in a great oak chair. He caught it by the blade; it sliced across his palm and dark blood mingled with the dust on the floor. The fleas feasted. His heart stopped. The man stirred. He was a giant of a man, covered in a great bearskin, with wrinkled bleached white skin, leathery lips, and a grey beard that stretched to the ground and across the floor of the cave. This was him, Owen Lawgoch, the man who should have been king. His heavy eyelids did not open, but his hand reached out for his sword. Clutching at the air, it grabbed hold of Dafydd's shirt, pulling the wretched boy towards him. He could smell the rancid breath. Lips moved. 'Is it time?' Dafydd did not know whether he was in a dream, or whether he was about to be torn limb from limb. He placed the sword back in the man's hand, and he shuffled back into his hibernation. As Dafydd turned to leave, he saw gold and silver coins all over the table. Was this the wealth he was promised? He filled his pockets, and the old conjurer shook his head. A wolfhound that lay by Lawgoch's side stirred, and the boy with pockets overflowing was gone.

Dafydd returned home along the old drovers' road, and emptied his pockets onto the table in front of his bewildered father. 'Well, there's a use for poets after all,' he said, and returned to his sheep. Dafydd returned to bed, but he was restless with only poetic thoughts to occupy him, and he felt the pull of the cave at Craig-y-Ddinas. He thought about all that gold. If only he'd taken more, he could have more wealth than he could ever wish for, more than he could ever need, he could write a slim volume and publish it himself. Chivalric stories about how King Arthur returns to his court at Llanbadarn Fawr and seeks the wooden cup from Nanteos that is reputed to be the Holy Grail. He would be the talk of Bloomsbury.

The following morning he was back on the old drovers' road. He found the hazel tree, walked down the steps, and everything was as he left it, a cave full of snoring, stinking men. He filled his pockets and left. Each time he visited the cave he pocketed a little more, until one day he took a sack, and as he filled it, he picked up a coin with an engraved image of one of Lawgoch's ancestors. The wolfhound stirred and slavered, Lawgoch turned in his sleep, the cave echoed with croaking voices, 'Is it time?'

'No,' shouted Dafydd, but every man in the cave was shaking a thousand and a half years of sleep from their weary eyes; fleas and dust filled the air, and one by one they stood, clutching their swords, surrounding the boy, ready to sever his head, but the stench of body odour in the air was enough to kill him alone. He was about to faint when a voice said, 'Stay your hands. This is but some worthless creature. A poet.' The lumbering men took the sack from his hands, and returned to their slumber. Lawgoch took hold of Dafydd's scrawny neck and lifted him up. 'Never wake me again without good cause, boy,' he growled, and dropped him on the dusty floor. Dafydd dragged himself to his feet and ran home, to be greeted by his father. 'Where's our gold? Have you spent it, useless boy?' When Dafydd returned to the tree he could find no entrance to the cave. Father and son were at loggerheads once more, a conjurer shook his weary head, and the world was deprived of one more poet.

OWAIN LAWGOCH AT GILFACH YR HALEN

One fine summer's day, a shepherd at Gilfach yr Halen found that one of his sheep had wandered onto the beach and had disappeared into a cave. He followed it into the cave until he reached a large room lit by lamps hanging from the ceiling. There was a long oak table running the length of the room, with ten strong sleeping men seated around it, and at the far end was a tall hairy man sitting in an ancient high-backed Welsh stick chair. His left arm was folded under his head and his right arm was stretched across the table, covered with a red birth mark. He held a great sword with the emblem of the Welsh princes, and in the middle of the table was a heap of gold coins with images of ancient French kings. The shepherd grabbed as much money as he could and hurried out of the cave before the men woke up, forgetting about his wandering sheep. He told the village about his find, and they went to the cave to fill their pockets, but they never did find the cave with Owain Lawgoch and his soldiers, who are still sleeping, waiting to return when their country calls them. They may be surprised when they do awaken, as Gilfach-yr-Halen is now a Holiday Village, full of caravans and chalets.

THE WICKEDEST MAN IN CEREDIGION

In a mud-walled cottage on the banks of the River Teifi just outside Lampeter on the road to Llanwen, lived an old God-fearing farmer named Siôn Philip. Stout and upright, stubborn as a mule, he laboured all hours on the land which had been worked by his father and grandfather before him, for as long as the old man could remember. The land was rich and fertile and it was kind to old Siôn and his wife. It gave them bread from the wheat he grew, milk and cheese from the cow, woollens from the sheep, meat from their ugly pig, and eggs from the hens. The land was his heart and soul, his very body; the man and the mud were the same. He had found his heaven on the soil of the earth.

Above the farm, with a vista of the whole of the Teifi Valley, was the stately home of Peterwell, a grandiose castle with four towers and a sense of domination over all it surveyed. It was the property of John Lloyd, and on his demise from an attack of nerves, it was inherited by his brother, Sir Herbert Lloyd of Maesyfelin, and this is when the trouble started.

You see, Sir Herbert had a reputation. Although a handsome man, he was generally believed to be the wickedest man in Ceredigion. Ask anyone in the taverns or fields, and they would tell you that he was vain, greedy, arrogant, brutal, vindictive, ruthless to the defenceless, a bully, a tyrant who lined his own pockets, an inveterate gambler, and a man of evil machinations and devilry. Perhaps not surprisingly given his qualifications, he was both the local MP and magistrate. As Justice of the Peace, he made and broke his own laws with grim regularity, flinging the poor and the defenceless into jail in order to extract fines, while as MP he indulged himself in as many fashionable vices and extravagances as Regency London had to offer, and was a sycophant at the court of King George III. He ran a house so full of servants and a stable so full of horses that he was frequently in debt, although if anyone dared to present him with a bill, he would force them to eat the blue paper it was written on and then beat them with his riding whip until they swallowed it. He was so popular that one farmer threatened to run him through with a pitchfork while another accused him of being a scoundrelly dog. Both were imprisoned. A friend once said kindly of him, 'He will never cease to persecute. It has become second nature to him.'

So Sir Herbert moved in, bringing with him not only his worldly goods, but also most of the stone from his old house, Maesyfelin, which he demolished and transported to Peterwell. Sir Herbert was fond of his old house, as it had been cursed by vicar Pritchard of Llandovery after his son Samuel died there from suffocating between two feather mattresses during a night of debauchery and an argument over love. Samuel was placed in a sack and thrown into the Towy, and on discovery of his body, his father declared, 'The curse of God on Maesyfelin, on every stone and root therein.'

Sir Herbert continued his life of cruelty and indulgence in his new home, while his wife Anne left for the solitude and peace of Llanddewi Brefi. Sir Herbert liked Peterwell. He liked its grandeur, its power, its curse, and most of all he loved the grand vista of the beautiful Teifi Valley so panoramically displayed from the flower garden on his roof. He was thinking that he should have one of those damnable artists paint it for him, Gainsborough maybe, or that young Rowlandson; he could be rather rude and would be cheaper. However, there was a small piece of grit in Sir Herbert's jar of Vaseline, for right smack bang in the middle of his aesthetic vision was a small mud-walled hovel with a badly thatched roof standing in an untidy field containing a few straggly beasts, including an unpleasantly ugly pig.

Old Siôn and his wife were quite happily unaware of Sir Herbert's thoughts, until one day a servant from the big house placed a bag of gold into the old farmer's hands and informed him that the Master of Peterwell was buying his cottage and land. Old Siôn gave polite thanks and returned the bag, saying the land was not for sale. The servant was sent back with more and more gold and each time Old Siôn returned it. Then a carriage trundled into the farm, and Sir Herbert stepped out in his fine clothes with his chest out and a riding whip in his hand. Old Siôn faced him with his face like a grim poet, with a straight back and a chicken under his arm. Sir Herbert offered the old man more gold than he could imagine, enough to buy him a handsome house in Lampeter and employ a pretty maid to care for him for the remainder of his days. Old Siôn politely declined, saying that the land could not be exchanged for mere gold, and that he, his wife, his forefathers, and his ugly pig had roots in the soil; the land was his soul, it was where his spirit breathed. He would be as a seedling left out to dry in the hot sun. He had all he needed, and no amount of gold could offer him more. The land could not be sold. Sir Herbert was completely baffled by this, and the pig was chewing his frock coat, so he roared away, alarming the chickens so much they refused to lay for a week afterwards and had to be chucked under their chins by Mrs Siôn.

It's like tickling trout, thought Sir Herbert, I've got to be more subtle with the silly old fool. So he invited Old Siôn up to the big house, and sat him at the kitchen table in front of a hearty meal of fine ale, cured meats, feathered fowl and exotic fruits, with servant girls to cater for his every whim, followed by a guided tour to allow him a peek at the grandeur that awaited him. When Sir Herbert joined him and asked how he had enjoyed his repast, Old Siôn explained that he had eaten nothing, for it was too rich for his digestion, and he found the surroundings an affront to his Methodism. This was too much for Sir Herbert. He had never encountered a man who was immune to wealth and ostentation. All that prattling on about no one truly owning the land. Stuff and nonsense. And how dare he invoke Methodism! Sir Herbert went to chapel too. He'd paid for some five-star preachers to come to Lampeter to put the fear of God into the scum. He had tried being nice; it was time for Old Siôn to meet the wickedest man in Ceredigion.

Sir Herbert hatched a plan. He had a valuable prize black ram, and he ordered his two most loyal henchmen to lock it away in an outhouse out of sight. He then put word around that his ram had disappeared, and he sent his servants to search the country-side for it. When he was satisfied everyone knew he had been robbed, he ordered his two henchmen to take the ram down to the mud-walled cottage, place a ladder against the wall, heave the ram up the ladder on to the roof, tie a rope round its midriff and lower it down the chimney. This done, Sir Herbert called the constables and informed them that he knew who had stolen his valuable black ram. The chief constable of Lampeter burst into old Siôn's cottage to find him staring at the ram who was sat by the hearth, grazing on some herbs that were drying in a bowl. The constable arrested the old man on suspicion of being a sheep rustler and he was taken before the magistrate in Lampeter, none other than Sir Herbert. The magistrate offered him a deal: sell the land or be sent to trial as a sheep stealer. Siôn explained once again that the land could not be sold because no one man owned it; it would be easier to sell Siôn himself. Sir Herbert ordered him to be placed in the stocks to await justice. He was then marched the 25 miles to the court of Great Sessions at Cardigan where he found himself facing a judge and jury, all of whom were servants and employees of Sir Herbert. He was found guilty and sentenced to be hanged at the gallows on Banc y Warren. Old Siôn's wife's screams were never to be forgotten by anyone who witnessed the execution.

Within a few days Sir Herbert had bought the old man's farm and evicted the old lady. Delighted with his now perfectly aesthetic view and the success of his plan, he tried it again on a farm called Maesypwll, this time with a valuable carpet instead of a ram. However the farmer knew what had happened to Old Siôn and quickly poked the carpet into the fire, and was sat warming himself by a roaring blaze in his hearth as the constable burst in.

Sir Herbert, meanwhile, after several nights gambling in a den in London, was found one morning with a gun in his hands and his brains blown out. His many debtors now served their blue papers without fear of a whipping, but Sir Herbert had died owing a fortune. The law stated that a body could not be buried until the debts were paid, so his coffin was left at Peterwell under guard, and after several months the house began to smell. His servants, in desperation, served the bailiffs drugged ale and whisked Sir Herbert off to the graveyard. Sir Herbert still refused to lie down, and his irascible ghost was seen on many occasions, striding around his flower garden trying to whip the heads off the daisies.

TWM SIÔN CATI,
THE TREGARON TRICKSTER

Thomas Jones of Fountaingate, Tregaron, was a poet and scholar; a thief and lawbreaker. He was a Protestant, living at the time when Catholic Mary I was on the throne, who received a pardon on 15 January 1559 on the accession of Elizabeth I. Later the same year, the vicar of Tregaron, Morgan Davyd, marched to Jones' house with a heavily armed gang laden with knives, swords, staves, pitchforks and pikes. He stabbed Jones with a knife, set dogs on his livestock, and assaulted his serving maid. Clearly, Jones had upset the Church. In 1607 he was accused of forging the will of Thomas Rhys Williams, whose wife he had married only a month after

Williams' death, leaving a smell of foul play. Jones himself died in 1609, leaving three heifers, twenty sheep, a feather bed to his son John, and a long list of debtors. His wife Joan married within the month, and presumably the vicar danced a jig of joy.

Thomas Jones became known as Twm Siôn Cati, the Welsh Robin Hood. Stories about Twm were already being told in Tregaron when a pamphlet appeared in 1763, entitled 'The Joker, or Merry Companion'. Twm and a gentleman entered into a wager that Twm could not steal a sheep from the gentleman's servant while he was carrying the animal along the road to the next village. Twm left a shoe in the road and the servant saw it lying there, but as there it was only one of a pair he left it to the tramps. Further down the road he found the second shoe, so he tied the sheep to a tree and ran back to collect the first shoe. He picked it up, but when he returned, the second shoe had gone, and so had the sheep. The servant threw the first shoe to the roadside in anger, where Twm collected it and walked off with a pair of shoes and a sheep. Later, the servant was carrying another sheep to the village when he heard a sheep bleating. He thought it may be the one he mislaid earlier, so he tied the sheep to a tree and went looking for the bleating sheep. Twm made off with the second sheep, and was away with two sheep and a pair of shoes.

Twm was riding to Welshpool when he met a man who said, 'That's a fine horse you have there.' Twm told the man it was a magical flying horse, and could perform many tricks and illusions. The man bought the horse and asked Twm to show him the tricks. Twm explained that the horse could fly like the wind and disappear, so he climbed onto the horse's back and galloped away before the man realised the trick.

Twm was held up by a highwayman who demanded his bag. Twm explained that his master had asked him to ensure the bag was not stolen, but he didn't want any trouble, so he invited the highwayman to shoot a couple of holes in Twm's cloak to suggest that he had been in a fight; then the bag could be handed over and no harm done. The highwayman liked Twm's dishonesty and shot into the cloak, emptying his pistol. Twm then pulled out his own pistol, shot the highwayman dead, and robbed him of his booty and his boots.

The final story in 'The Joker' is probably the best known. A poor man from Llandovery had been sent by his wife to buy a porridge pot. Twm explained how he could acquire one cheaply. He told a stallholder that there was a hole in one of his pots, and the stallholder held it above his head to see if he could see light shining in. Twm pulled the pot down over the man's head, and was away with another pot while the stallholder tried to pull it off his head.

Soon more pamphlets were published about the Tregaron Trickster, some literary creations, others collections of folk tales. The story of the Welsh Robin Hood first appeared in 1828 in *The Adventures and Vagaries of Twm Siôn Catti* by T.J. Llewelyn Pritchard.

Twm had a feud with another highwayman, so decided to teach him a lesson. He disguised himself in rags and tatters, found the skinniest of mules with its ribs showing, loaded its empty panniers with seashells, and rode to the place where his fellow highwayman worked. The highwayman appeared but Twm, quick as a blink from a crow's eye, threw the panniers over the hedge. The highwayman dismounted and scrambled after the money, while Twm leapt onto the highwayman's white stallion and was away with the wind, along with the robber's loot stashed into his own panniers.

Twm was courting the Lady of Ystrad Ffin, serenading her beneath her window at night. She was pretending not to be interested, so he took hold of her pretty white hand and kissed it, but she pulled her hand away. Twm told her he would sever it from her arm unless she married him. She refused, so he took his knife and drew blood from her wrist. She agreed in order to keep her hand, suggesting that Twm the Trickster was not always the loveable rogue as commonly thought.

One market day, Twm decided on a trick. He made a fake tail and attached it to a bull which had a short tail. The owner of the bull came along and Twm invited the man to buy it. The man said that Twm's bull looked suspiciously like his own, only with a longer tail. Twm protested, and chopped off the fake tail along with the end of the real one, causing a little blood to drop. The farmer was now satisfied the bull was Twm's, but refused to buy it as it had been mutilated. Twm was outraged, and with the support of the crowd who had been watching, he forced the farmer to pay up. Twm made off with the money, and the tail, in case he ever needed to steal another short-tailed bull.

The farmer came hunting Twm over the theft of the bullock. He arrived at Twm's mother's house and knocked on the door. An old beggar man in rags answered the door, and the farmer asked if Twm was in. The beggar replied that he was, and offered to hold the man's horse while he went inside. The man entered and the beggar leapt onto the farmer's horse and was away like greased lightning, discarding the rags to reveal that he was Twm. He rode to the farmer's house, explaining to his wife that her husband was in serious trouble and needed money urgently, and had sent Twm on his horse to fetch it. She loaded his saddle bags with money and Twm rode away with the farmer's horse and money, off to London where he sold the horse and made merry with the ladies.

In the late 1940s the *Western Mail* published a daily cartoon strip called 'The Adventures of Twm Siôn Cati', he was popularised on TV in the 1978 series *Hawkmoor*, and then as an animated cartoon on S4C. In 2009 Tregaron celebrated Twm's 400th anniversary by unveiling a statue of him. Everyone in the town will tell you of their modern-day Twm, Dafydd Wyn Morgan, who tells the stories, dresses in character, leads guided walks to the cave at Dinas Hill near Rhandirmwyn where Twm hid from his pursuers, and keeps alive the memory of the old trickster.

SIÔN CWILT, THE WILD MAN IN THE PATCHWORK COAT

In Ceredigion, if you could build a house in one night and have smoke billowing from the chimney in the morning, then all the land a stone's throw around was yours. It was called a *tŷ unnos*, a one-night house. One stood at Synod Inn, halfway between the smuggler's cove at Cwmtydu and the Ffynnon Bedr home of Sir Herbert Lloyd, MP, Justice of the Peace, and wickedest man in Ceredigion. It had been built by a mysterious man, said to be a relative of Sir Herbert, a man named Siôn Cwilt.

There were stories about Siôn. He had built his own house because he was too big to fit in his mother's house; he was called Cwilt because he wore a patchwork quilt for a coat; or he was gwyllt, a wild man; he was also known as Siôn Sais or John the Englishman (a son was born to a John Quilt in nearby Llanina in 1758); he kept Sir Herbert supplied with brandy; though the best story of all is that so little is known about him, yet the locals drank his health.

One night in 1797, a ship from Roscoff pulled into the bay at Cwmtydu with a cargo of brandy. With the help of strong men and twenty fine horses, the kegs were unloaded and the brandy stowed away in caves along the coast. Over the next few weeks the folk of Cwmtydu had smiles on their faces and their noses were redder than usual. Sir Herbert Lloyd was particularly happy. Then a man named Daniel Ifan was caught selling bottles of brandy in Llangrannog, and was hanged as a smuggler. There were protests in New Quay; troops were brought in, the coast was swarming with excise men, and the liquor vanished into thin air, as did the wild man in the patchwork coat.

But that is not the last of Siôn. The spot where he is thought to have built his *tŷ unnos* is named Banc Siôn Cwilt. The writer T. Llew Jones wrote many children's adventures about him, which have already passed into folk memory. Perhaps a smuggler is an unlikely man to have a school named after him, but in Synod Inn children attend Ysgol Bro Siôn Cwilt.

THE GREEN MAN
OF NO MAN'S LAND

Although the Gypsies were itinerant, some planted roots in North Ceredigion. The Wood family settled along either side of the Dyfi estuary, and in 1877 storyteller and fiddler Matthew Wood was recorded telling tales on the seafront in Aberystwyth with his mother Saiforella, who is buried in the town. Matthew told his stories in Romani, simply and at great speed, almost too fast to be heard. He was a romantic figure in his prime, with mystical deep-set eyes, aquiline nose, sensitive mouth and long black curls reaching to his shoulders. He often got so carried away by the drama and emotion that he would identify himself with the hero.

Matthew's great uncle, Jeremiah Wood, known as Jerry Bach, was harper to the Prices of Gogerddan and lived at the mansion along with his sister, Black Ellen, who was known as a witch, wise woman and storyteller. Black Ellen smoked a clay pipe and pointed it into the air for emphasis. She knew 300 stories, many of such a length that they could not be told in one night. To test the audience's attentiveness she would call out 'Choiya' (boots) and expect the response 'Xolova' (stockings). If the response wasn't quick enough she would stop and never finish, or she would ask what the last word she had said was, and if she was given the right answer, she would continue. All nine of Jerry Bach's sons were harpers, the most famous being John Roberts of Frolic Street in Newtown, who gave regular recitals in Aberystwyth, and was buried in Llangynfelin Churchyard in 1867. He told tales such as 'Jack and the Golden Snuffbox' and 'An Old King and his Three Sons in England'.

Johnnie MacDonald was born into an Irish traveller's family in Shropshire around 1860. His father was sent to prison for murdering a man, so he was brought up by his grandmother, then travelled with his uncles and their cart, working as a tinsmith, a word he preferred to tinker. He won his wife in a fight at Trelech, and she eventually died giving birth to their fourth child. A barmaid from a pub in Aberystwyth found Johnnie and his children living in a tent on Penglais Hill. They married and settled in a small cottage in Llandre where they had five more children and adopted another. He set up a workshop where the Spar now is, and told Irish folk tales in exchange for being read the *News of the World* by his son, Tom, who wrote his father's story in 'The White Lanes of Summer'. He described Johnnie as a proud man who never accepted more for a job than it was worth, as bald as a potato with a fringe of salt-white hair.

The stories the Gypsies told were rooted less in the Welsh landscape than the itinerant world of fairy tales. The Woods' stories are closer to the *Arabian Nights* than the Mabinogion, while John MacDonald's were from Irish travellers. This is one of Matthew Wood's stories.

Lo, there was once a young miller called Jack, and he was a great one with the cards. He was sharp of nose, pointed of chin, with a face as expressionless as a mask. No one could beat him.

One day a man walks in and challenges Jack to a game; nothing strange in that except this man is green from top to toe. He has skin the colour of limes, hair the colour of grass, eyes of deep green water, a waistcoat speckled as a courgette, and pantaloons of broccoli. The man bids everything he has, including his castle, and Jack wins. The man asks for a rematch, and Jack loses. The stranger speaks. 'I am the Green Man who lives in No Man's Land. If you can find my castle in a year and a day, it is yours; otherwise I will hunt you down and cut off your head.' Jack thinks. A year and a day is a long time and a castle should be easy to find. 'A deal is a deal,' says Jack, and the Green Man is gone.

Jack returns to his milling and forgets the game. But as winter comes on and there is less work in the mill, he falls to thinking about losing his head. He wraps himself in furs, saddles his horse and sets off to look for the castle. He comes to a cottage and knocks on the door. A little old woman answers and Jack asks for a bed. 'Come in, young man,' she says, 'there's a bed for you.' He asks if she knows the Green Man of No Man's Land. 'I know no Green Man, but if a quarter of the world knows, then I will know in the morning.' Jack puts his horse in the stable and takes to his bed. In the morning the old woman climbs up a ladder onto the cottage roof, blows a horn, and a quarter of the world stands outside the cottage. She asks them if they know the Green Man of No Man's Land, but no. She blows again and a quarter of the world's birds come and she asks them if they know the Green Man, but no. 'Jack,' says the old woman, 'I have an older sister, she may know of the Green Man. Take my horse, place this ball of wool between his ears and he will take you to her.' Jack saddles the horse and is away like lightning.

He arrives at the old woman's older sister's house. She greets him, 'It's long since I saw my sister's horse. Come in, young man, there is a bed for you.' He asks if she knows the Green Man of No Man's Land. 'I know no Green Man, but if half the world knows, then I will know.' Jack puts the horse in the stable and takes to his bed. In the morning the old woman climbs up a ladder onto the cottage roof, blows a horn, and half the world stands outside the cottage. She asks them if they know the Green Man of No Man's Land, but no. Half the world's birds come, but they do not know the Green Man. 'Jack,' says the old woman, 'I have an even older sister and she may know of the Green Man. Take my horse, place this ball of wool between his ears and he will take you to her.' Jack saddles the horse and is away.

He arrives at the old woman's older sister's even older sister's house. She greets him. 'It's long since I saw my sister's horse. Come in, young man, there is a bed for you.' She knows no Green Man, 'but if the world knows, then I will know.' In the morning the old woman climbs onto the cottage roof, blows a horn, and the whole world comes. She asks them if they know the Green Man, but no. She blows again; all the world's birds come, but they do not know the Green Man. Again she blows, and an eagle flies in. 'Where have you been, lazy bird?' asks the old woman. 'With the Green Man who lives in No Man's Land,' replies the eagle.

'Jack,' says the old woman, 'saddle my horse, place the wool between his ears, follow the eagle; he will take you to a great lake. On the lake will be three swans. Hide in the rushes by the water's edge; the birds will come to the shore and shake off their feathers. While they are bathing, take the third swan's feathers. She will find you, for she is the Green Man's daughter. Ask her to take you to the Green Man's castle. No matter what she says, do as she asks you, and do not take no for an answer.'

Jack sets off on his journey, the horse following the eagle, until they come to a lake with three swans. Jack hides in the rushes and the swans shake off their feathers to reveal three naked girls who bathe in the lake. Jack's eyes pop out of his head, but he remembers to steal the third bird's feathers. The girls return. Two dress and fly away, but the Green Man's daughter finds Jack. 'Give me back my feathers,' she says. 'Only if you carry me over the lake to your father's castle,' he replies. She places Jack on her back and swims across the lake to a great castle. Jack knocks on the oak front door. It opens and there stands the Green Man of No Man's Land. 'You have found me, Jack? I was looking forward to chopping off your head. You're not a bright boy, one of my daughters has helped you, but which one?' Jack says nothing. 'That will cost you five tasks, Jack. First, clean my stable.' The Green Man shows Jack the stable and gives him a shovel. It is the filthiest pigsty he has ever seen in his life, piled with pooh of every shape, colour and consistency. He takes the shovel and throws a steaming pile out of the window. Three come back at him. One green, one brown, and one the colour of curry. He throws another shovelful; three more come back, all the colour of curry. Once more, three more, one hitting him in the face. He throws the spade down in a tantrum, stamps on the ground three times, sits down and sobs. Youngest Daughter appears. 'Jack, stop crying, go into the house and eat. Not curry. Do not tell my father I was here.' Jack obeys, eats jam and bread, and when he returns the stable is spotless. When the Green Man sees, he says, 'One of my daughters has helped you, but which one?' Jack says nothing. The Green Man takes him outside and points to a vast forest. 'Jack, your second task. Fell all these trees by lunchtime.' Jack takes an axe and fells a small spindly birch tree. The sweat is pouring off him like honey; he throws the axe down and weeps. Youngest Daughter appears. 'Jack, stop weeping. Go into the house and drink. Not honey wine. Do not tell my father that I was here.' When he returns, all the trees are felled, and the Green Man says, 'One of my daughters has helped you, but which one?' Jack says nothing. The Green Man shows Jack a pile of wood. 'Jack, your third task. Build me a barn by day's end, roofed with a thatch of feathers.' Jack spends two hours catching a wren before it escapes without leaving a feather, and he's bawling like a baby. Youngest Daughter appears. 'Jack.'

'Yes, I know,' and when he returns, the barn is built. The Green Man says, 'Jack, your fourth task. In the middle of the lake is a glass mountain. On the peak you will find a bird who lays only one egg. Bring me that egg.' Jack stands at the edge of the lake, too tired to cry. Youngest Daughter removes her shoe and wishes it into the shape of a boat. He climbs into it and she sails him to the glass mountain. She transforms into a white ladder, and tells him he must step on every rung, not to miss one. Jack climbs and finds the egg at the top but in his eagerness, he steps over the last rung. There is a cry of pain and the ladder changes back into the girl, but her little finger is broken. 'Do not tell my father,' she says. He presents the egg to the Green Man, who knows his youngest daughter has been there.

'Jack, your final task is to choose your bride. My daughters will fly three times around the castle in the shape of swans. Find my youngest daughter and she will be yours.' Jack watches the swans in flight, all as white as snow, all with yellow beaks, all with orange feet, all beating their wings with a humming sound. He notices one of them has a broken wing feather and he points. 'There is my bride.'

And that is why you will see Jack walking round with his head still attached to his body.

THE WAR OF THE
LITTLE ENGLISHMAN

There has long been a tradition of Englishmen moving to Wales, acquiring land and building castles. The Welsh also have a tradition, of fighting for the land they love. It is part of their soul – they belong to the earth beneath their feet and carry it with them wherever they go, like the mud on their boots. They call it *hiraeth*, a yearning, a longing, a word that barely translates into English.

So it was in 1815 – when absentee landlords and mining speculators were buying the commonly owned land in north Ceredigion – that John Hughes, the surveyor appointed to enclose the commons around Mynydd Llanrhystud, found himself surrounded by thirty odd-looking old women armed with dripping pans. They showed him the hole where they kept their surveyors, and Mr Hughes, quite understandably unnerved, diplomatically left, never to go near mountains, dripping pans or unshaven old women ever again. Soon there were 200 of them on the mountain, watching, and staring, and looking fetching in their frocks.

So the fairy tale begins. In 1819, a gentleman from Lincolnshire, Augustus Brackenbury, bought several hundred acres of common land on Mynydd Bach, for he had decided to build himself a castle. He hired a cheap workforce of local men to build a road to allow access on and off his land, and a cottage to live in while his castle was being designed. He was unsure what to make of the locals; they seemed polite enough, even though they spoke a language he didn't understand. They were a little unnerving, for they had a habit of staring at him through dark furrowed eyebrows. They were good at staring. Men and women. Especially the children. Sheep, too.

Dafydd Ifan, the blacksmith, lived in a small damp cottage named Bwlchymynydd near Llanrhystud. Dafydd had a son, a dark shaggy-haired boy named Siaci. An inquisitive boy, Siaci Ifan could stare better than any boy on Mynydd Bach and he could blow a pibcorn louder than any cow could bellow. He and his father cut peat to sell in Aberystwyth and raised a few animals, as the soil was too thin and waterlogged to grow healthy crops. Earning a living was hard; men had not returned after the Napoleonic Wars, some had fled for America in pursuit of hope and dreams, and now the land they worked had been sold to a rich man.

The Englishman began to build his cottage while Siaci and his friends watched. They couldn't take their eyes off him. Siaci saw a grand man in a silk hat, a velvet waistcoat, carsimer trousers and white socks, and assumed he must be a lord. He watched his lord and followed him everywhere. The lord spoke to him saying, 'Go away, ragamuffins,' but the children said nothing; they just stared because he spoke in a language they didn't understand.

Soon the walls of the lord's cottage were built, the roof timbers were in place with just the roof tiles to add and he went to bed that night feeling most satisfied. In the morning, he awoke to find his cottage had burned down to the ground, and there was Siaci Ifan standing behind him, staring. 'Did you do this, guttersnipe?' Siaci said nothing. The lord grabbed the boy by the ear and dragged him to see the Justice of the Peace. The justice explained that the men and women of Mynydd Bach were upset that he had been allowed to build on their land. The lord said it was his land, he had bought it with good money, but the justice explained that it had been bought from the king, who had in turn taken it from the locals. The lord argued, so the justice fined him 2s 6d for arresting an innocent boy. The lord was confused as he walked away from the court. He was building a nice new cottage that would look much smarter than the tin-roofed or shabbily thatched hovels that the locals lived in, and yet he was being treated like a criminal. As he stood in the drizzle, a stone hit him between the shoulder blades. He turned round to see Siaci and his friends staring at him. He decided to rebuild his cottage, and this time he would employ watchmen.

The cottage was rebuilt, walls and roof timbers in place with only roof tiles to add, when a mob approached the house and Dafydd the blacksmith asked the watchmen to leave. They didn't, so the next night the mob came again, this time with staves and clubs, and some of the watchmen fled. On the third night, the remaining watchmen were greeted by the mob armed with pitchforks and sticks. It wasn't that they were armed that was so terrifying; after all, the watchmen had guns. It was that every man was dressed in a skirt, an apron, a blouse, a shawl, and a bonnet, and all of them had lamp-blackened faces. Confronted with an army of transvestite Welshmen, the watchmen ran, leaving the lord on his own in the middle of his roofless cottage. He raised his gun and ordered the mob to go, but then realised how ridiculous it would look if he shot a man in a frock. He lowered the gun, and they burned the cottage down to the ground. The lord refused to leave until his coat buttons became as hot as coals and he was almost roasted alive.

The lord was apoplectic, and hurried back to see the Justice of the Peace, armed with a list of names he had seen the previous night. The wheels of justice cranked into action. No one came forward to give evidence, so he put up posters offering rewards for information leading to the arrest of the arsonists, but as the posters were in a language they didn't speak, the locals tore them down. Undeterred, the lord decided to build a third cottage for himself in the woods, in the hope that the mob were so busy hiding from justice, they wouldn't notice. The walls were built and the roof timbers were put in place, and down it burned.

Three times he'd tried to build his cottage; three times it had burned to the ground. This was war. Gathering stone from the hillside and importing timber at great expense, the lord began building cottage after cottage, thinking the damnable ladyboys wouldn't be able to burn them all down. However, he underestimated the strength of a Welshman in a frock, and those they didn't burn down, they knocked down with pickaxes. Exhausted, red in the face, and with a large hole in his bank balance, the lord returned to London to lick his wounds and fume to anyone who would listen.

Three years passed, and the lord had a plan. He decided he was wasting time trying to build cottages. He would simply build his castle. He returned to Mynydd Bach where little had changed; the gorse was in bloom, it was drizzling, Dafydd the blacksmith was no richer, and there was Siaci, 14 now, still staring. This time the lord was ready. He had imported stone and timber, he brought labour in from Shrewsbury, and he persuaded the militia to leave their barracks in Aberystwyth to protect him while his mighty castle was being erected. By April 1826 the castle stood at the foot of the hill at Troed y Foel. It was big. A great wall enclosed a tower with narrow windows and doors for archers – not that anyone used longbows any more. It was surrounded by an 8ft moat with a drawbridge. He called it Castell Talwrn, or the Cockpit. Let's see them try to get in here, he thought. He employed a local woman named Lisi to clean for him.

The locals gathered and secretly thought it looked quite impressive, so instead of resorting to arson, they took the lord to court. They accused him of allowing one of his men to strike an old man with the butt end of a musket causing a cut to his lip, threatening to throw a woman in the moat, robbing a fatherless boy of his wooden shoes, throwing a cart into a bog having first released the horse, stealing turf from a cottage roof, demolishing the turf stacks of the poor, failing to appreciate that they had a right to cut turf on the Mynydd as their fathers and grandfathers had done, not to mention general threatening, bullying and rule by gun law. The lord was ordered to pay a shilling here and half a crown there.

On the night of 23 May 1826, word went round that the lord had gone to Aberystwyth on legal business and would stay the night. Dafydd was ready, Siaci blew his pibcorn, and the people answered the call. They came from Llanrhystud, from Llangwyryfon, from Llanilar, they came on foot through marsh and meadow, bog and butterwort; some said 600 came, some 1,000. What a sight, men dressed in skirts, aprons, blouses, shawls and bonnets, with lamp-blacked faces. They surrounded the castle. There were four watchmen left inside, every one of them stout-hearted in war, but in the face of a transvestite mob, they fled. Only Lisi the housemaid was left, and when she saw the white shining eyes staring at her through blackened faces, she let down the drawbridge and in they poured.

They took the bedding, furniture, and paintings, and threw them in the moat. When the castle was empty, the boys of Trefenter moved in with their hammers and pickaxes, and by the time the sun rose there was nothing left of Castell Talwrn but a heap of stone and a clogged up moat.

The lord was in tears. The militia from Aberystwyth were sent for, Dafydd and Siaci were arrested and transported to Cardigan Gaol, though during a halt for a drink at the New Inn near Llangrannog, Siaci escaped. Dafydd was hauled before the Great Sessions. However, as the Sessions were held in English, and the defendant and all but one of the jury spoke only Welsh, Dafydd was unexpectedly cleared due to lack of understanding as to what was going on. The lord, however, sued for compensation and the people of Mynydd Bach had to pay higher taxes. Finally, he built a small cottage named Cofadail Heddwch, a monument to peace, and the war ended. The lord sat in his castle in the air watching Dafydd and Siaci cutting his peat for their fire. Who won? Who knows?

Shortly after, the lord left for London to begin a new business dealing in salt. All that remains is the road, Lon Sais (the Englishman's Road), close to another monument, Captain Henry Morgan's Trench, built the length of Cwm Wyre down to the sea to launch a boat the captain had built on the Mynydd. Many locals left for Ohio to escape famine and find new hope, leaving their ruined houses behind them. One village was left deserted, save for an idiot boy who was stoned to death by folk from other villages. Siaci Ifan became the sexton and gravedigger at Llangwyryfon, lived to the age of 87, and he told the story of the War of the Little Englishman to anyone who would listen. More visitors came in the 1920s to hold exclusive parties on the island at Llyn Eiddwen, where the locals later built a monument to four of their local poets. The land of Mynydd Bach is still mostly common. If anyone won the war, it was the land itself.

And the men-women? Well, they returned during the Rebecca Riots to protest against road tolls; they turned up in the Ceffyl Pren, a form of folk justice where people made effigies of those who offended them and paraded them through the streets; they were in the Mari Lwyd, with the horse's skull that was paraded around New Quay at New Year; and in late Victorian photographers' shops where bearded men were captured in heroic poses wearing Welsh women's costume. Every Saturday night in Aberystwyth, a few hairy male students are still seen wandering the streets dressed as nurses. They are 'The World Turned Upside Down'.

THE DEVIL'S BRIDGE

In the second half of the eighteenth century, the minister and Protestant Reformer Edmund Jones, known as 'Prophet Jones,' set off on an itinerary around Wales, searching for evidence of the works of the Devil. He neglected to make enquiry in Ceredigion, as he felt sure that there was as much devilry there as everywhere else. How right he was. Shall we dance a tango around Tregaron?

Let's begin in Llanarth, where the people of the parish believed the Devil was trying to steal their music by making off with the church bells. One fine day the vicar was walking through the churchyard reading his Bible when he heard a noise in the steeple, as if someone was trying to ring the bells. He climbed the spiral stairs of the church tower to find the Devil sawing his way through the bell ropes. He was black all over, with a long forked tail, horns and cloven feet. The vicar opened the Good Book, sprayed holy water over the Devil and the bells, and spoke. 'In the name of God and Christ get out, filthy devil, foul creature, wince under thy chastisement, leave evermore the House of God in Peace.' The Devil was already dripping with holy water and had no wish to listen to a dreary sermon, so he leapt out of the window, landed on a stone in the churchyard and hared away as fast as his cloven hooves could carry him. The stone he landed on bears four marks: the Devil's Footprints.

Near Aberaeron, a stone marks the spot where a fisherman was told that if he wished for riches, he should cast his line in the river on 29 December, the day the Devil would be fishing. So there he was, sat by the river, catching fish by the bucketful. He gutted them on the bank side to make them lighter to carry home, and as the innards tumbled from the speckled belly of a trout, something glistened. He wiped the blood away and found that he was holding an ivory black ring. He placed it in his pocket, thinking this was the riches he had been told of. Greed was tickling him, so he cast once more. He felt a shiver. There was someone behind him. He tried to turn his head but he was rooted to the spot. He heard

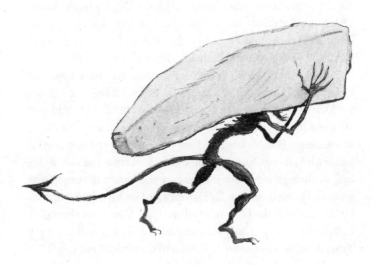

a dark rasping voice, saying, 'You have my ring. Return it and you shall have your freedom.' The fisherman was petrified and his arms wouldn't move. The Devil reached into the pocket, pulled out the ring and was gone. The fisherman couldn't move, a prisoner inside his own body. He was found by friends, frozen stiff; the only part of his body that twitched were his terrified eyes, until he finally turned to stone.

Inland we go, following the river towards Llanddewi Brefi. Early in the 1800s there were two ladies, baking cakes and growing flowers for the church, just reaching that difficult age when teenage rebellion creeps back, showing itself by dressing in bright silks with moons and stars, red streaks in their hair rather than blue rinse, and thoughts of toy boys in turbaned heads. One Sunday morning they took Holy Communion, and held the bread in their mouths till the end of the service. They began to walk around the church walls, for they believed that if they did this nine times, they would invoke the Devil, or at the very least see the one they were to marry. On the sixth circumference their hearts beat a little faster; on the seventh their stomachs churned; on the eighth they shook with fear; but their legs would not stop and on the ninth they were in hysteria; and then, from the hole by the porch where they had spat out the communion wine, he appeared, the Devil himself, Satan, Old Nick, Beelzebub, in the form of a frog. They fed the frog the bread from their mouths, certain they had sold themselves to the Devil and would become witches.

Prophet Jones, in his search for devilry, may have bypassed Ceredigion, but he did tell stories about the infamous conjurer, Sir Dafydd Llwyd. It was widely believed that Sir Dafydd had obtained his supernatural powers by selling his soul to the Devil. In exchange, Old Nick was to have possession of the conjurer on his death bed, providing he could drag him from the side of his bed, or through a door, or if his corpse was buried in consecrated ground. On his deathbed, Sir Dafydd asked his friends to drag him by the feet over the bottom of the bed, push him out through a hole in the wall, and bury him beneath the church wall at Ysbyty Ystwyth, so he was neither in nor out of consecrated ground.

In the late nineteenth century, the villagers of Penparcau awoke one Christmas morning to find footprints in the fresh snow. Some said it was a headless dog (who we will meet later), others said St Nicholas, but the footprints were like no other; neither beast nor man, cloven-hoofed and large, and made by a creature who walked on two legs, not four. They followed the tracks through fields and woods, and over walls, in one straight path. The only conclusion they could come to was that it was the Devil who walked through Penparcau that Christmas.

Back to the most famous story of devilry in all Ceredigion; the story of the Devil's Bridge. In the village of Pontarfynach, there lived an old woman, called Megan Llandunach. She was standing on top of the gorge with the waterfalls of the River Mynach far below, and the sound of crashing water in her ears. She was wailing into the wind, sobbing uncontrollably, a small shabby mongrel howling beside her. She became aware of a man, so she turned and there stood a monk, dressed in grey robes with a hood pulled over his face so his eyes shone. From beneath his cloak she could see his feet were cloven. He spoke, 'Why do you cry so, my dear?' She dried her tears. 'Because my cow has wandered, and she is on the other side of the gorge, and I am too weak and feeble to climb down and up the other side, or to walk to the source of the river to cross.' The Devil told Megan that he would build her a bridge so she could retrieve her wayward cow, providing she gave him the soul of the first living creature that crossed the bridge. She dried her tears, wiped a dewdrop from her nose, and agreed, while the Devil dreamed of beef in his soup. He set to work; he carried the finest stones from all parts of Wales and Ireland, pausing only once to be disturbed by the preaching of the vicar of Llanarth.

The Devil was tramping over Trichrug Hill with a great stone around 4.5m high and his feet were sore, so he sat down on top of the stone, lit a cigarette, poured himself thick black coffee from his thermos, and sang a rude song about twenty-four virgins from Inverness at the top of his voice. Walking up the road towards him was the vicar of Llanarth who he had encountered at the church, still with his head in the Good Book. Oh bother, thought the Devil, not another sermon. He pressed down on the rock and launched himself into the air and away, leaving behind his fingerprints, though some say he left two smooth circular imprints behind him, the Devil's Buttocks.

Soon he had built a fine bridge across the gorge, and he showed it to Megan. The old woman whistled her cow to stay, pulled an old loaf from her pocket and threw it across the bridge and the shabby mongrel ran after it. The Devil threw his head back, exposing his skull and deep eye sockets, and let out a howl that made blood freeze, before setting off on his way with the soul of a shabby mongrel on a piece of string trailing behind him. Not only conjurers can outwit the Devil.

There are many stories of devils building bridges over rivers to capture souls, but this one is not the ancient fairy tale it seems. At the end of the eighteenth century, tourists were arriving in mid-Wales, inspired by the beauty of nature and art. Thomas Johnes had built the Hafod estate nearby, to create a romantic image of the wild woods where waterfalls were aesthetically arranged to please the eye. To encourage visitors, the name of the village was changed from Pontarfynach to the darker and more inviting Devil's Bridge, and an old folk tale was adapted to explain the legend of the new name.

Around 200 years before the Devil built his bridge, there lived a man called Bat or Bartholomew, otherwise known as publican Matthew Evans of Tregaron. He had three children – two boys and a girl – known as Plant de Bat, or Plant Matt, meaning Matt's children. They grew into thieves, hiding out in a small cave in Devil's Bridge by day, and robbing by night. The cave was only big enough to allow one in at a time. They used a glove as a passport, and could defend the cave against hundreds. Here they lived for many a year until they murdered a gentleman for his wealth and his friends took dogs to hunt them, who sniffed out the cave. The two boys were hanged, the girl burned, and the riches given to the church.

While prosperity arrived in the form of tourists in search of the wild woods, the people were impoverished. The Enclosures Act took their land, the lead mines were closing and road charges became financially crippling. By the end of the nineteenth century a railway was built from Devil's Bridge to the sea at Aberystwyth, to bring holidaymakers in from the bustling seaside town and provide a transport link for the mines. But the navvies who worked on the railway were anything but angels. Catholics from Ireland and Italy fought on the streets of the picturesque little village. In 2007 the BBC announced plans to make a film about the disturbances between Italian and Welsh miners at nearby Frongoch Mine, which historians claimed were greatly exaggerated. The film was left unmade and the trains take visitors to see the bridge, while the Devil watches on, smiling, and clutching his shabby mongrel.

THE HEADLESS DOG
OF PENPARCAU

A few years ago, a boy in Penparcau, near Aberystwyth, saw a dog that had no head. As he stared at it, it simply faded away. The Headless Dog has been seen many times, and there are two quite different folk tales that tell its story.

MAELOR AND HIS SONS

There was a giant named Maelor who lived with his three sons Cornipyn, Grugyn and Bwba in a great castle that covered all the land around Pendinas and Penparcau. Maelor liked to sit on top of his hill, Dinas Maelor, and survey his territory, watching nervously in case any neighbouring giant came to take his land from him. His brow was furrowed, for there were many greedy giants. There was

Samson, who was cutting his corn when his flail broke in two. The long part landed in Llanbadarn Fawr, and in anger he threw the rest of the flail into the churchyard, so creating the two standing stones currently in the church exhibition. Samson was so big that he left a grain of sand from his shoe as a rock by the roadside at Goginan. There was Cawr Crug Mawr, who became King of the Ceredigion giants by throwing his quoit from Trichrug Hill over to Ireland; Wyti Bwli, who lived by the Chalybeate well between Llyn Eiddwen and Llyn Fanod and led the men of Trefenter in a battle against the men of Llanrhystud, between the giants of the land and the giants of the sea at what is now Blood Lane; Howel, Llyphan and Pysgog who had three sorceresses for wives and who were slain by Arthur's nephew Gwalchmai; and there was the cannibal giant of Caerwedros who was eating all the locals until St Cynog slew him after luring him out by hanging a corpse on a gallows, though not before the giant had bitten a slice from Cynog's thigh.

Maelor watched the sea to the west, for fear the invading Irish giants were wading across Cardigan Bay. He watched the mountains to the north for fear Rhitta of the Beards was coming to rob him of his chin stubble. He watched the hills to the east for fear the three terrible robber-giants of Cwmystwyth came pillaging and plundering, and he watched the floodlands to the south for fear Ysbaddaden Bencawr, the chief of the giants, was watching.

One day, Maelor was striding round his lands when he was attacked by his enemies at Cyfeiliog. He was bound in chains and they were about to cut off his head when he pleaded for a final wish, to blow his horn three times. On the first blow, his hair and beard fell off. On the second blow, the nails fell from his fingers and his toes flew into the air, and on the third blow the horn shattered into a thousand pieces.

Cornipyn was sat at Cefn Hiraethog when he heard the sound of the horn and he was overcome with grief and longing for his father. He saddled his horse and set off to rescue Maelor, with his dog trailing behind on a leash. He rode with such speed that his dog could not keep pace with him, and as he was about to leap across the valley, the dog's head was severed by the leash, at a place called

Bwlch Safn y Ci, the Pass of the Dog's Mouth. The horse landed at Ol Carn y March, the Steed's Hoofmark. The poor dog died in vain, as Cornipyn was killed trying to free his father, Maelor was executed, and Grugyn and Bwba were hunted down and killed.

The dog still haunts the summit of Pendinas searching for its severed head, sniffing around the 20ft column that was meant to have a statue to the Duke of Wellington on it. The statue was never made, leaving the column as headless as the dog.

THE HEADLESS DOG OF PENPARCAU

On the land between the River Rheidol and Pendinas, before the caravan park and the housing estates were built, there lived a sheep farmer and his daughter. He was in the middle of a good lambing season when his daughter was taken ill, so he rode into Aberystwyth to fetch a doctor. He left his faithful sheepdog to protect the birthing ewes and keep watch over his sick daughter. Aberystwyth was growing in size, encroaching on the farm, and there had been young lads hanging around, up to no good. When he returned he sensed that something was wrong: the stillness of the air as he approached, the smell of death, and finally the sight of every single one of his newborn lambs decapitated. He feared for his daughter and rushed into the house to find her lying in bed, covered in blood, barely alive. By her side was his sheepdog, tongue lolling, gasping for breath, also spattered with blood. With little thought, he picked up the great woodcutter's axe and with one blow took off the dog's head, staring at the twitching body, oozing life.

The doctor walked into the scene of carnage, and tended to the daughter. The farmer stood by the bed saying little; his head bowed, lost in a dark place, his addled mind uncomprehending. In time the daughter recovered and told her father what had happened, and it made his blood run cold. Shortly after he left to fetch the doctor, she heard the sounds of frightened bleating sheep; she rose from her bed and looked out the door to see a great beast rampaging through the flock, biting and snapping at anything that moved, severing the heads from the lambs. Seeing the girl, it ran towards her and lunged at her, clawing at her, and at the same moment the sheepdog leapt onto its back and began tearing at its throat. The dog clung on, dragged the beast towards the door, drove it from the house, lifted the girl into bed and waited by her bedside until her father arrived home.

From that day on, at every lambing season, the dog returns to the fields around Penparcau to keep guard on any lambs that need protection and any child who is unwell. It was seen just before a man went to fight in the First World War.

This story has a striking similarity to the legend from Beddgelert in Snowdonia, when a prince returns and slays his dog after thinking it has killed his baby, although the dog had actually killed a wolf that was attacking the child. The Beddgelert story was invented at the end of the eighteenth century as a ploy by the landlord of the Goat Hotel to bring tourists into the village and part with their money. The Penparcau story, however, is clearly part of a longer tradition.

The Cŵn Annwn and the Beast of Bont

The *Cŵn Annwn*, the Dogs of the Otherworld, were the hounds that accompanied the Kings of Annwn on their wild hunts. In folklore they were sent out to seek corpses, and the sight of them – or the sound of their bark – was a portent of death. The brother

of a farmer near Llanarth heard them on the road to Bronwen; another was heard at Llangeitho; a *cŵn cyrff* (or corpse dog) was seen at Ystrad Meurig; two folk returning from Chapel at Ysbyty Ystwyth on a mild sultry evening kept to the side of the road as the 'little dogs' went by. They described them as *cŵn toili*, speckled phantom funeral dogs, or *cŵn mamau*, mother's dogs. Rhosygarth was haunted by a Gwyllgi, a dog of darkness, which was said to have the head of a dog and a body more like a cow. In Cwmtydu, a man frightened by stories of mad beasts heard a noise at night and, thinking it was some monster, shot his neighbour's cat. Before rabies was eradicated, a child's greatest fear was to be bitten by a rabid dog.

In 1981 many sheep were mutilated near Pontrhydfendigaid, and cat-like prints were found nearby, giving rise to stories about the Beast of Bont. Locals said it was a black panther, released into the wild after the government tightened the law on keeping dangerous animals. It struck again throughout the 1980s, the mid-1990s, and most recently in 2012. There have been sightings and sheep have been attacked in Talybont, Borth, Horeb, Tregaron, Lampeter, Dihewyd, Goginan, Penparc, and Devil's Bridge. A rival beast has been named the Panther of Pantgoch. Folk believe there are several of them and that they have been breeding for many years. They follow the hedgerows from one area of the county to another, so remain largely unseen. The Beast of Bont's fame has led to it having its own online game on the BBC Wales website where you can help Sabrina, the protagonist, escape its clutches. So far there have been no sightings of werewolves, although the *Cambrian News* reported that a boy had apparently heard one howling in the woods in 1995.

THE TALE OF THE FAITHFUL SHEEPDOG

A farmer and his wife, Dafi and Catrin Rees, lived at Cefngwyddil Farm near New Quay. Every Saturday Dafi rode his old grey mare to Carmarthen on business, while his sheepdog Teifi loped along a few steps behind. One Saturday the north wind blew, it was bitterly cold and a bank of dark cloud was gathering over Banc Siôn Cwilt.

Dafi knew it would snow before nightfall, so he set off early with Teifi behind, barking wildly and running from side to side. Before he even reached Carmarthen the snow was falling heavily, drifting against the hedges and filling the ditches. He went about his business as fast as he could, filled himself with food and a couple of drinks, wrapped himself in all the clothes he had, and turned for home.

The snow fell and the wind blew and Dafi was sleepy from the drink, but the old grey mare knew her way, and soon they reached the hill at Ffostrasol. Heavier and faster the snow fell, and he slid from his saddle in a heap; there was a crack and a shriek of pain and he slid down a bank into a snowdrift. The old grey mare bolted towards home and the dog began to lick his master's face. His leg was broken and he couldn't move for the pain, but he knew that if he stayed there he would die of cold. In that moment a feverish heat overwhelmed him and he passed out.

The old grey mare reached home and Catrin's heart sank at the sight of the riderless horse. She called the servants. They roused the village; they took lanterns and a search was made but there was no sign of Dafi. All that night they ploughed through the snow, fearing no living soul could survive the freezing cold of that night. By dawn's rosy fingers they found him. He was lying in the snowdrift where he had fallen, his leg shattered, his faithful dog Teifi lying sprawled on top of him. They were both alive. The warmth of the dog's body had been enough for them both to survive. They were lifted onto biers and carried back to Cefngwyddil, where Catrin warmed them by the fire and fed them warm soup while the doctor set Dafi's leg. The following day, Teifi was back at work tending the sheep: the dog who had saved the life of his friend.

THE TRANSVESTITE
WHITE LADY OF BROGINAN

'One of the most astonishing reflections on the mind of man is the absurd effects of a disordered imagination. To this we must attribute the invention of ghosts,' said Samuel Rush Meyrick in his *History and Antiquities of Cardiganshire* in 1810. Curious, then, that over 200 years later, almost everywhere in Ceredigion has a ghost story.

There is the drowned harper of Llandyssul; the ghost cat of Ystrad Meurig; the little yellow spook of the valley at Troedyraur; the bicycling ghost of Blaenpennal; the stone-throwing ghost of

Tregaron; the black pirate ghost of Llanafan Bridge; the acrobatic ghost of Llanfihangel-y-Creuddyn; the ghost pig that haunted the road below Tynbedw; the combustible cat of Rhosmeherin; the headless dog of Penparcau; Jac y Raca, the mariner of Aberporth; the crying child who wandered Talybont after being found at the bottom of a mineshaft; the unrepentant forger and monk who haunts Strata Florida every year on 14 December; the Rhosygarth dog of darkness; the murdered man of Newcastle Emlyn Rugby Club; the photographed ghost of the Ty'n Llidiart tavern in Capel Bangor; the ghostly landlady of the George Borrow Hotel in Ponterwyd; Mrs Jones of Aberbodcoll still searching for the money she left behind after her heirs demolished the pigsty looking for it; the horseman in the red scarf who appeared and disappeared near Lledrod; the ghost of Dorothy Gale in the Coliseum Cinema; the wheel of fire which hung over the grave of a pedlar on Pendinas murdered by the local butcher and his son; the French sailor in the 1840s, seen by his lover in Aberystwyth at the very moment he perished when his ship sank off the coast of Spain; the chimney sweep who walks the tavern garden near Llanafan where he was buried when he drank a quart of ale; a woman who haunts Llanina after her head was severed by her husband who suspected her of infidelity; Dr Rogers of Abermeurig who was drowned with his servant in the Great Storm of 1846 and appeared to the servant's brother to tell him not to grieve; Thomas and Jane Johnes of Hafod, who wander the woods giving misleading directions to tourists; and the Green Lady of Teifi with her long dark hair in plaits, guarding a mound full of treasure.

And there are the White Ladies who haunt Devil's Bridge, Llangunllo, Llwynshiwan, Crosswood, Talybont, and Tre'rddol. Broginan is the birthplace of the poet Dafydd ap Gwilym, and was said to be haunted by the ghost of a strikingly unusual Ladi Wen. She was tall and handsome, dressed in lustrous white with long brown hair flowing over her shoulders, her face hidden by a silken veil that covered the stubble on her chin. For the white lady was a man, who stomped on the stairs in great boots and wandered around slamming doors. If no one paid him any attention he would illuminate the entire house before vanishing in a ball of fire. He was particularly fond of disturbing courting couples. One evening when the family had gone to chapel, a young man named Evan came wooing the servant girl, and to cool his ardour she told him about the cross-dressing ghost. As Evan was laughing, the white lady appeared, clutching a comb and paper, with his five o'clock shadow exposed. He wandered around the room then beckoned the terrified and bemused couple to follow him up the stairs into a dark back room, where he pointed to a corner under the low roof. Evan saw a parcel wrapped in a woollen sock wedged behind a rafter. He opened it to find a wad of money, and the transvestite white lady vanished, never to be seen again.

In around 1890, a young man dressed himself in a white sheet to pretend he was the white lady of Crosswood Park, so frightening the horse pulling Dr Hughes's trap that it bolted, overturning the trap and almost killing the good doctor.

CORPSE CANDLES AND PHANTOM FUNERALS

Portents of death come in many disguises, from birds entering a room to howling dogs, knocking or wailing, hearing the singing of hymns, or *canwyll gorff* (corpse candles) – lights that move slowly through the night till they rest over a house, a sign that death will shortly visit. They also appear indoors as haunted candles. A young woman came to stay with her aunt in Aberystwyth for Christmas. She was awoken in the night by the clock striking one and saw a blueish light in the room. The candle was alight, so she blew it out and huddled back under the bedclothes, but the candle lit again. She blew it out once more, and again it lit, and a third time. She spent the night shivering beneath the eiderdown, not daring to open her eyes. In the morning, she told her aunt's servants, who all agreed it must be a corpse candle and so it was, for a few days later – just after Christmas – her aunt died.

A young girl lived in a remote cottage near the derelict lead mines at Cwmystwyth. On one of those still dark evenings, she was standing in her doorway when she saw a procession winding its way towards her. It was a phantom funeral, a *toili*. The people were a little smaller than most, dressed in old clothes, white and shining in the dark. As they passed the cottage, just a few feet from the girl, one of them stopped, stared at her, bowed three times and the procession walked on. Three days later, the girl's father died. A woman in Cwmtydu was sat by her fire when a *toili* passed the house; she followed it to Wig Cemetery, and a few days later a real funeral passed the house. Hafod was well known for sightings of *toili* and *canwyll gorff* as well as phenomena such as dogs howling at night and birds pecking at windows by day. A postman described being buffeted by unseen hands as he walked along the road to Hafod Church.

THE GHOSTS OF ABERYSTWYTH PROMENADE

Aberystwyth must be the most haunted place in Ceredigion, possibly because the student population delight in scaring the wits out of each other. The university hall of residence Cwrt Mawr Block H is thought to be haunted, and many have seen or know of the Lady of Craig Glas, a spectral woman who floats around Constitution Hill. The Lady is thought to have fallen to her death from the cliff edge, and now prevents others from suffering the

same fate, although she did once appear in the games room of the Cliff Railway restaurant.

In 1971, a young couple were seen running to each other on the prom, floating a foot above the ground before embracing, descending to the beach and disappearing into the sea. They are believed to be a young couple who had been drowned at the base of Constitution Hill after being trapped by the tide. A ghostly soldier in a khaki uniform has also been seen on the prom, not to be confused with Aber's legendary street bard, Bob the Poet, dressed in his Spanish Civil War uniform.

During the renovation of Alexandra Hall at the foot of Constitution Hill, the workmen reported seeing ghostly figures moving down corridors and entering rooms, but when they were followed into the rooms, they had vanished. The wages clerk for the mainly Slovakian, Polish and Cardiff workforce noticed that names he didn't recognise were appearing on the workforce list, and wondered if they were adding the names of the ghosts in order to claim extra wages from the company which they were then pocketing.

THE BOTHY BOOK

On 17 February 1856 Margaret Hughes of Nantsyddion near Ysbyty Cynfyn gave birth to the first known quadruplets in the world, Margaret, Elizabeth, Catherine and Isaac Hughes. By the end of March all had died of typhus and were buried in the same grave in Ysbyty Cynfyn. Ten days later, two more children and their father were dead. The locals had tried to help by leaving them gifts of food and money by the well, dipped in vinegar to avoid passing on the plague.

Margaret survived the fever and stayed at Nantsyddion before madness took her to Carmarthen Asylum, where she is thought to have killed herself. The vicar refused her request to be reunited with her children and her husband, for a suicide would not be allowed in consecrated ground, so she was buried outside the church walls. Later the churchyard was enlarged to include her, and she now lies close to the vicar who rejected her. The churchyard walls are almost round, and contain five large standing stones, giving the impression that the walls were filled in between the stones.

They are said to be old standing stones, though some think they look a little more like gateposts.

Nantsyddion is now a bothy, open for weary walkers to rest the night. There is a Bothy Book for visitors to write in, which contains descriptions of an apparition or presence. It is described as a kindly soul, like a mother fussing over her children. On the wall, written in candlewax, is the name Margaret.

SIACI CLIFFORCH AND THE SLIMY HAND

Siaci Clifforch, a plump bumbling man, was walking home one moonlit night at Michaelmas when he heard a voice from St David's Well near Henfynyw, crying for help. 'A relative must help me,' said Mair, 'if I fall I will spend a thousand years in bondage; I won't hurt you, give me your hand. Sin, ball of fire, 'tis true on my word.' A green hand dripping with slime reached out of the well; Siaci gripped it tightly and pulled but the hand was so slimy that it slipped from his grip and there was a thud. The voice said 'You have failed me, man of Clifforch. A thousand years in chains will I spend, poor is Mair.' Siaci called down the well but there was no answer and he never heard a voice from the well ever again.

Another tale tells of blind Gwen, who lived by the same well and whose sight was returned to her by St David. There is a children's game called *y bwci yn y ffynnon*, the ghost in the well, where children tell their 'mother' there is a spook in the well sharpening a razor, but the child playing the mother pooh-poohs the idea until the *bwci* chases her and tries to chop off her head.

NANTEOS

Ghosts are so closely entwined with stately homes that estate agents have been known to include them in their sale details. Nanteos has more than most. The Jewel Lady is thought to be Elizabeth Powell, a former mistress of the house who hid her jewellery on her deathbed; a phantom huntsman haunts a culvert in the grounds; a phantom horse and carriage pulls up at the main entrance in the night; the Grey Lady, thought to be Miss Corbett (future wife of a member of the Powell family, owners of Nanteos), appears with a candelabra to signal the death of the head of the house; the ghost of the harper Gruffydd Evan who played for the Powells every Christmas for sixty-nine years still plays in the music room and the woods; and there is a ghost that haunted a BBC film crew; ghosts in Ceredigion seem to be particularly fond of haunting BBC film crews. Nanteos was also the home of the remains of a small wooden cup which has poured out many stories. It was said to be the Holy Grail, the Eucharist Cup from which Jesus drank. It was rumoured that it was made of the olive wood from the Calvary Cross; that it was kept by seven monks at Strata Florida Abbey who were in hiding from Henry VIII; that it could cure anyone who drank from it; and that Richard Wagner was so inspired by it he wrote *Parsifal*.

The cup is a mazer bowl, made of wych elm, which would have been kept in religious houses as a drinking vessel. It first appeared at Nanteos in 1876 at an exhibition of relics and antiquities organised by the Cambrian Archaeological Society. They had carried out a dig at Strata Florida, which was owned by George Powell, romantic poet, friend of Swinburne, and also owner of Nanteos. The cup is still in the possession of the descendants of the Powells, who left Nanteos in 1960. It contains slips of paper, written by people who were cured after drinking from the cup. Stories are still being told: apparently the cup at Nanteos is a fake; the original was bought by a rich American and resides in a bank vault in Shrewsbury. Sadly, Wagner never came to Ceredigion to see the chalice.

The Aberystwyth Arts Centre Artist in Residence Ghost

Aberystwyth Arts Centre appoints three artists in residence every three months, and they share a house near the hospital. In 2012 one of the artists believed the house was haunted by a ghost, a fairly kindly ghost. The haunting was believed to have been caused by a previous artist in residence who had lived in the same room and had been working on a project to create a ritual that would return the Devil to Aber.

CROOKED
BETI GRWCA

In a tiny thatched mud-walled cottage on the slopes of Banc Penrhiw near New Quay lived an old humpbacked woman named crooked Beti Grwca, who was thought to have dealings with the fairies. Young people came from all over to visit her, because old Beti knew how to make love potions, and how to sell them to ambitious lovers.

One day the nursemaid from Plas y Wern called to see Beti, with her young charge, a little boy named Cedrig. At the same time, the maid from Rhyd-y-Ferwig farmhouse arrived with a baby wrapped in a shawl, a girl named Elinor. Old Beti gave the two maids their regular doses of love potion, and decided on a little mischief. She poured a drop of water taken from the well at Pistyll-y-Rhiw that she kept in an earthenware jar onto a leaf and gave it to Cedrig and Elinor, spoke some strange words and pronounced that the two little ones would be in love for the remainder of their days. Off she went, cackling to herself, as mischievous old souls do in fairy tales.

Eighteen years later, Cedrig, the heir to the Plas y Wern estate, was to wed Gwen of Cilbronnau, while Elinor was working as a maid on her parents' farm. Old Beti Grwca was even more crooked of back, still selling her love potions, and as full of mischief as ever. Elinor, remembering nothing of Beti, went to visit the old woman for a potion, and Beti, not recognising Elinor, sold her one. At that moment, a dark-haired lad called at the mud-walled cottage to ask for a drink of water, took one look at Elinor, fell instantly in love, and invited her to marry him. Beti, a little surprised at his barefaced cheek, asked who the young man was, and he said Cedrig. She asked the girl if her name was Elinor, and she said yes. The old woman explained that she had given the two youngsters the same love potion eighteen years before. The youngsters needed little encouragement, and met secretly for a year, until they knew they were truly in love. Cedrig told his father he could not marry poor Gwen, and the old man stormed and raged, and told the boy that Elinor was nothing better than a poor farm girl with no dowry. Elinor's parents thought Cedrig's family was stuck up and that money wasn't everything. The marriage was forbidden and arguments raged, until one calm evening as the red sun was setting, Cedrig and Elinor took a boat across Cardigan Bay to Barmouth, where they married. Like many before and many to come, they honeymooned by the Mawddach, and returned home to find the old Squire of Plas y Wern had worked himself into such a state over his son's adventures in love that he was as stiff as a board in his deathbed. Cedrig inherited the estate and filled the house with children. Poor Gwen of Cilbronnau, however, was last seen paying a visit to crooked Beti Grwca, in the hope of finding a man who would be true.

THE BOGEY OF THE RHYD

A few generations ago, there was a mischievous bogey who lived in a farmhouse by the Rhyd Bridge at Gilfach-yr-Halen. Everyone in the neighbourhood knew about the bogey, and they all lived in fear of crossing the bridge or passing the farmhouse, because the bogey was very good at the tormenting. It would hide in a twilight place just after nightfall, wait for a traveller on the road, emerge from the shadows, and then it would begin taunting, biting, scratching, kicking and pinching until the poor victim was black and blue and bruised all over. Many ran for their lives; others shook with fear, some fainted clean away, and the worst thing was, they couldn't even see their tormentor.

One evening a young jack-the-lad named Siôni was whistling his way home after an evening canoodling on the couch with his sweetheart at Gilfach-yr-Halen, when he reached the old Rhyd Bridge. He was so loved-up that he clean forgot about the bogey and started to cross the bridge.

He saw in the shadows a queerly shaped creature, dribbling and oozing and holding a lighted rush candle in its hairy little hand, and hopping on its heels from side to side in a curious and threatening manner. Siôni realised he was face to face with the bogey of the Rhyd. He turned to run back across the bridge but the bogey was still in front of him. Wherever he looked, there was the bogey: sometimes in front, sometimes behind, kicking and pinching him towards the Cwm Cottage at Gilfach. He tried to run for the safety of the house, but the bogey was behind him, driving him as a dog would a sheep, through mud and brambles towards the brook. Siôni found himself on the high rock at the top of the waterfall and as he peered over the edge into the darkness he knew with grim certainty that he was about to die. He turned and stared the bogey in the face, and as he did so, the bogey threw back its head and let out a blood-curdling screech that froze the hearts of the night owls. He held the rushlight over his head three times, blew out the light, laughed manically and melted away into the darkness. Siôni was so bruised that it took him hours to crawl back to the farmhouse and weeks to recover, though he was pampered with the kisses and cuddles of his sweetheart.

GUTO OF CWM GIDO AND THE LITTLE RED MANNIKIN

There was once a kind-hearted bright-eyed boy named Gruffydd, known as Guto, who had one leg longer than the other, for at the end of the short leg he had a club foot. The boys in the town laughed at him and called him Big Foot, but the girls liked his wide smile and warm heart and loved to stroke him. He spent his days sat by the little stream at Tyddyn-y-Cwm, watching the dippers and the wagtails, for the birds did not laugh at him,

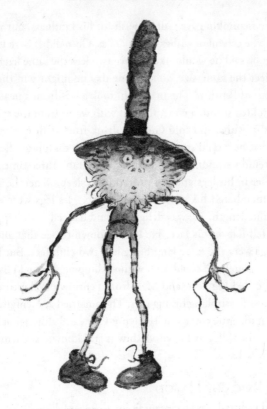

and he could dangle his feet in the cool water, and watch how the ripples were so much larger from his club foot.

One day Guto was sat near his home, listening to the rattling stream singing harmonies to him, when he heard something behind him. It sounded like cursing. Swearing. He looked round and saw something struggling to escape from a bramble patch. He thought it must be a hare, so he hobbled over to free it, and found himself face-to-face with a little mannikin about 1ft high, 2ft if you took his pointed hat into account, dressed entirely in red, with large piggy ears and long pipe-cleaner legs. As he struggled he was being torn by the thorns, so Guto carefully took hold of him, pulled all the brambles away, stood the little mannikin on his feet, and told him to be more careful or he might fall into the nettles.

The mannikin gave Guto a wish for his kindness, but warned him to be careful of wishes in fairy tales. Guto didn't have to think twice; he said he would like to have two legs the same length and two feet the same size, so that one day he might win the heart of Mari of Penrhiw. The mannikin took a leaf from a nearby oak tree, folded it into a cone, filled it with water from the spring at Pistyll-y-Rhiw, and told Guto to drink from it three times and see what he would see. The little mannikin disappeared, as they so often do at moments like this. Guto drank three times, felt a shudder in his legs and fell promptly to sleep. When he awoke, he remembered his wish, and stood up. His legs were exactly the same length. He was delighted, and danced with happiness, then fell flat on his face. He looked down to see that although his legs were the same length, he had two club feet. But he was happy enough; he could walk without limping, he could live with being called Big Feet, and Mari from Penrhiw developed quite a fondness for stroking his big toes. They married at Henfynyw and lived at the little cottage at Tyddyn-y-Cwm and although it is now a ruin, the valley at Pistyll-y-Rhiw is still known as Cwm Gido, or Lovers' Lane.

THE BWCA OF HAFOD

Hafod Uchtryd was an elegant house that was falling into disrepair because the old couple who lived there failed to care for it. The owner of the local lead mine in the mid-1800s, John Paynter, decided that he would like to live there, and soon the old couple became troubled by a *bwca*. Tormented, they left, and Paynter moved in. Talk was that Paynter himself was the *bwca*.

Soon after he moved in, the maidservant complained that the *bwca* was still there. It cuddled her from behind and fondled her in the dark. Tongues still wagged, but Paynter protested that he too was plagued by the *bwca*. It appeared to him in the form of a beautiful woman and tried to seduce him. Then the *bwca* turned itself into a pig and chased him into the river. So he called on the services of a *dyn hysbys* from Brecon, and paid him £100 to remove the *bwca*. After this, all went quiet.

In 1780 the house passed into the hands of Thomas Johnes, who built the great mansion of Hafod, and with it came the *bwca*. It liked nothing better than to pull the hair from the Master of Hafod's nose. It draped the master's great coat on the back of a chair, buttoned it up and placed three sods of peat on top for a neck with a hat above. The master, enraged at the impertinence, knocked the effigy down with a stick, only to have buttons thrown at him followed by the coat itself, and sometimes woke in the morning with a heavy chest laid across his feet. The *bwca* moved stones around the house, snatched candles away, locked fifteen people in a room, turned tables upside down, made potatoes leap out of a basket towards the ceiling as maggots jump out of cheese in hot weather, hit a parson over the head till he bled and kissed women in the dark (although never the mistress). It sometimes appeared to Mr and Mrs Johnes as a pig, and occasionally manifested itself as a beautiful woman wanting to be kissed, before changing back to a *bwca* at the moment of passion. It lived in the stables where it removed saddles from the horses, threw turf at the stableboys, and ransacked the place. Even when the house burned down, the *bwca* refused to leave. The master eventually brought in an exorcist from Oxford, who drew a circle on the ground. The *bwca* appeared in the form of a bull, then a bulldog, and finally as a fly that landed on the conjurer's book which he snapped shut, trapping the *bwca* forever.

22

Sigl-di-gwt

Long ago in the Pant Teg Farmhouse, there lived a woman and her pretty baby. The woman worked all hours to feed her child. Her fingers were red raw from washing, her back bruised from lifting and her breasts sore from feeding. At the end of each day she walked the fields to collect the wool that the sheep had rubbed onto the brambles and fences; she teased it and carded it and spun it into warm clothes for her little one.

One evening, the woman was spinning yarn by the light of a single candle, while her baby slept peacefully in her cradle by the hearth. She was singing a lullaby, 'Suo-Gan Gwraig Pant Teg', or 'The Woman of Pant Teg's Lullaby':

Mabi bach annwyl I, 'r goreu'n y byd
Sut bum I byw heb dy cwmni di gyd?
Fel rwy'n dy garu, fy mabi dinam!
Ti yw pri gysur a phlesur dy fam.

Lwli-bei, lwli-bei, cwsg nawr yn fwyn
Ti gei freuddwydio am adar acwyn
Blodau, a phethau bach tylsa' 'n y wlâd
Lwli-bei, cysga cyn delo dy dâd.

Mabi bach annwyli'r, hardda'n y wlâd
Cariad di fami, a thrysordy dâd
Ti yw f'anwylad, fy mabi bach mwyn
Ac yn dy berson, ymuna pob swyn.

Lwli-bei, lwli-bei, esmwyth bo'th hun
Mam sy'n dy wylio, amwylaf dy lun
Engyl a'th wylia, paid rhoddi'r un gŵyn
Lwli-bei, gorffwys yn dawel a mwyn.

Mabi bach annwyl i'r tlysaf mewn bôd
Cwsg tra bo'th fami yn nyddu a'i rhôd
Caua lygaid, a chymer dy hyn
Cwsg di yn dawel tra bôt ar fy nglin.

Dyna! 'Rwyn gwelad fod cwsg wedi dôd
Lwli-bei, lwli-bei, âf fy rhôd
Cwsg nawr yn esmwyth, fe wylia dy fam
Lwli-bei, lwli-bei, chei di ddim cam.

N.B. A translation of this lullaby appears on p.202.

As she sang, a little old lady walked into the room, dressed in a red and white striped frock, a red cloak, and black shoes with silver buckles. She peered through bottle-bottom glasses at the woman, squinted and spoke, without any how d'ye do. 'What would you give me if I were to spin all that wool for you, dearie? It'll take me but a few minutes, and you look so tired.' The woman was weary from a long day, drowsy from the embers of the fire, unsure whether she was dreaming, and she heard herself saying, 'Anything I possess would I give,' thinking she had nothing of value. 'The deal is done,' said the little old lady, and she licked her thumb with a raspberry tongue and placed the top joint against the woman's thumb.

The little old lady set to spinning and within a beat of the baby's heart, all the wool was spun. The woman was delighted and disbelieving, for this would have taken her hours and her finger joints would be aching and her eyes weeping. She thanked the little old lady and said, 'What can I offer you in return? A cup of tea or bara brith?' Quick as the blink of a crow's eye the little old lady pointed her finger and snapped, 'Your babi.'

The woman awoke. 'My baby, no, do not tease me, he is my life, my soul. I could never part with him. Undo your work, I would rather strain my sight.'

'A bargain is a bargain, sealed by the fair folk, it cannot be broken. For three days I will come, and on each day you will have three chances to guess my name. If you fail, as you will, your babi will be mine.' The woman blurted out, 'Mari, Megan, Meinir,' but the little old lady danced away cackling, as little old ladies do in fairy tales, singing over and over again, 'That's one.' The woman spent the day in disbelief, thinking it all a dream, but the following night the little old lady returned and asked for her name. The woman said, 'Ceri, Caryl, Cerys?' and the little old lady danced away cackling, gnashing her teeth, singing, 'That's two.'

The woman was shaking at the thought of losing her baby. The following day she walked around clutching him to her breast and muttering names to herself, as if she had lost her senses and was bound for Maudlin. She staggered down the slope from Pant

Teg to Cnwc-y-lili, and on until she came to Llanina Bridge, all the time talking to her baby. Should she pack her meagre belongings in a bag and run, should she stand her ground and fight for her child, or give up all hope and leap into the fast-running waters of the little river Llethi? She stood on the wooden bridge, singing her lullaby to the rattle of the water as it clattered over the pebbles, and she was so enchanted that she asked the stream to soothe her. In that moment she heard singing coming from the other bank. In a clearing in the trees she could see the little old fairy lady, dancing around her spinning wheel, surrounded by grey and pied wagtails, all flicking their tails, chanting 'Little she knows that Sigl-di-gwt is my name,' over and over again. The woman could not believe her ears. She turned and ran home.

That night the little old lady came. 'Well what's my name?' and she held out her arms and began to claw at the baby.

'Siani?'

'No.'

'Siriol?'

'No.'

'Perhaps it is Sigl-di-gwt?' said the woman firmly. The little old fairy lady turned green, then red, steam poured from her ears, spittle from her mouth, green goo from her nose, and she leapt up and down in a towering rage, turning the air blue with swearing. She stamped her foot three times, breaking the floorboards, and disappeared through the hole, never to be seen again.

THE COBBLER AND THE LITTLE RED MANNIKIN

In an insignificant cottage at Cnwc-y-lili, 400 yards from Llanina Bridge, lived a curious little cobbler, Deio by name, with his daughter Mairedi. Deio's wife was long dead and he had brought Mairedi up on his own having never remarried; not surprisingly, for he was short-tempered and squat, with a balloon for a head, a spongy red nose and a straggly white beard. But he was the best cobbler in New Quay; even the squire of Plas-y-Wern ordered shoes from him, though hard as he worked, he and his daughter were poor as church mice.

Mairedi was an intense, unsmiling girl, with eyes covered by a mane of thick black hair that had a mind of its own. She looked after her grumpy father, cleaned his workshop, dusted the spiders' webs, grew herbs in red pots, removed the jackdaws from the hearth after they had fallen out of their nests in the chimney and tidied up after he had thrown his tools at the wall in a tantrum. She earned a crust as a seamstress, taking in sewing from the neighbours and making samplers to hang on parlour walls to cover the cracks in the plaster. Late one evening, she decided to prepare breakfast for her father so she could have a little lie-in the following morning, before she collected her day's sewing from the neighbours. Brushing her black hair from her eyes, she laid the table with bread, cheese and milk, so her father could eat while he finished mending the squire's silken shoes. When Deio woke up, he found the squire's shoes were shining as new, placed neatly at the bottom of his old iron bed, and there was no breakfast on the table. Mairedi was intrigued,

Deio was hungry, and the squire was so pleased with the workman-
ship on his shoes that he paid the curious little cobbler double.

That night Mairedi laid the table again, with bread, cheese and
milk. In the morning Deio woke to find another pair of shoes had
been mended and placed at the foot of his old iron bed, although
this time the food had not been touched. This went on, night after
night. Now Deio was not a man to see a gift horse even if it chewed
his hat, and he grumped and growled and demanded to know what
was going on, but Mairedi pushed him up the rickety old stairs to
bed and told him not to meddle. However, Deio was determined
to catch a glimpse of his benefactor, so propping his eyelids open
with boot nails, he lay awake into the early hours until he heard
a sound at the bottom of his bed. He saw a little red mannikin
with long spidery legs and arms, dressed from head to toe in red
patchwork rags, placing a pair of boots at the bottom of his bed.

In the morning he told Mairedi what he had seen, and that the little mannikin's clothes were shabby and patched. He didn't wish to have a scruffy benefactor, so he ordered his daughter to sew a new set of clothes as a gift to spruce him up a bit. Mairedi told her father that this was the doing of the *tylwyth teg*. The mannikin might be insulted at the suggestion that his suit was raggedy, and her father should leave well alone. Deio threw a terrible tantrum and Mairedi was forced to spend the day making a little woollen jacket and corduroy trousers while he made a pair of tiny leather boots, and they placed the gifts at the foot of the old iron bedstead. Next morning, a pair of mended shoes were at the foot of the bed, but so were the jacket, trousers and boots. Deio was infuriated by this irritating little mannikin, and he tore the jacket and trousers to shreds.

The little red mannikin never came again to the limewashed cottage at Cnwc-y-lili. Mairedi knew the fairies were upset at her father for trying to see them, and that they preferred to gift rather than receive. However, the neighbours understood the kindness the father and daughter had tried to show the little mannikin. From that day on they gave the curious little cobbler all the work he needed, and his dark-haired daughter made a living as a seamstress, making quilts and embroidering pictures of little red mannikins for people to hang over the cracks on their walls.

THE FFOS-Y-FFIN GOBLIN AND THE ONE-EYED PREACHER

A boy – a bit of a blockhead – met three little men by the Rheidol and was taken through a cave into the land of the fairies. Here he was given an education, and on returning to this world passed all his examinations, was ordained by the bishop and became vicar of a parish north of Aberystwyth, possibly Eglwysfach, where R.S. Thomas was later to preach. However, not all encounters between the clergy and the Otherworld have been quite so rewarding.

At Ffos-y-Ffin, there lived a goblin who was very fond of the old tavern on the main road from Aberaeron to Llanarth. It was often to be found propped up on a wooden bench in the corner of the bar with a beer on the table in front of it, a clay pipe in its hand and a tale on its lips, for the goblin was a fine storyteller. It was particularly fond of the beer that was brewed in the shed outside the back door, which it liked to share with the village doctor, a kindly man who cared for all, rich or poor, smart or foolish, preacher or poacher.

One day, the doctor told the goblin that a popular preacher from the county was to give a sermon at the local chapel the following day. Now the goblin was not at all partial to preachers, particularly those important ones who always brought a suitcase full of pottery statues of themselves to be sold to the congregation at the culmination of the sermon and placed in the middle of the mantelpiece by the painting 'Giants of the Baptist Pulpit'. The only one the goblin admired was Christmas Evans, the one-eyed preacher, who at 17 was illiterate, uncouth, ill-dressed, had been stabbed, almost drowned, had fallen from a tree clutching a knife, lost his eye after being beaten up, used projections and shadow puppetry in his sermons, and whose hat was shabby from being filled with water for his old white horse, Lemon.

The kind doctor had offered the visiting preacher a bed for the night and the goblin was outraged. It decided upon the one thing that goblins do best: tormenting. The preacher duly arrived, and that evening before supper, the goblin set to work. The preacher was leading a prayer meeting by the doctor's fire, arms resting on a stool while he prayed. The goblin whisked the stool away so the preacher fell flat on his face in the hearth, singeing the tip of his nose. Then it rattled the poker and tongs against the fire, making an almighty clatter, and shook the dresser so the jugs and dishes leapt into the air and shattered on the flagstone floor.

The goblin also discovered it could frighten the preacher by leaping out in front of him, grimacing, gnashing his teeth, and gurning at him. The maid accidentally saw this and was so terrified that she dropped all the dishes she was carrying, breaking every one. Soon there was hardly any crockery left in the house.

The preacher barely slept that night, so in the morning he went for a peaceful walk in the woods to think on his sermon and calm his shattered nerves. He sat down in a buttercup meadow and was considering the beauty of nature when he was confronted by the goblin, dressed as a preacher. It pranced about in front of him, eulogising and pontificating, grimacing and gnashing its teeth, and the preacher could see it quite clearly now. It was 4ft tall, swarthy and quite forbidding, and although his theological training had prepared him for meeting such curiosities, this was very different to an evening with the Bible and a brandy in the cloister. Theory and practice were clearly two quite separate creatures, and he fainted clean away.

When he came to, the preacher decided there was only so much torment a mind could take and he prepared to leave for Aberaeron without delivering his sermon. He saddled his pony, bade farewell to the doctor and the servant maid, and rode away. The goblin, however, had not finished, and it leapt over the roadside hedge and onto the back of the pony. It spurred the pony on until it ran quicker than lightning, its legs unable to keep up with itself, with the goblin holding on to its tail. The preacher fell off, legs in the air, and landed in a ditch, where he found the goblin staring at him, grimacing and gnashing its teeth. He picked himself up, covered in mud, his nerves in tatters and his resolve shattered, and he walked away and never returned, preferring to preach to congregations more inclined to listen.

The Miracle at Nant y Moch

Nant y Moch chapel was flooded when a reservoir was built in the upper reaches of the Rheidol Valley to create a hydroelectric scheme, amidst much protest and the relocation of many people. In 1956, shortly after the scheme was announced, a local shepherd invited the Bayliss family from Wolverhampton and a farmer friend from Devil's Bridge to visit the chapel. The shepherd asked the farmer to enter the pulpit and read from the Bible, and then asked the Bayliss' young daughter to do the same. The little girl climbed the steps, and raised both arms into the air, to the astonishment of her parents, for she had been paralysed down her left side all her life.

Nant y Moch means 'Stream of Pigs', and is believed to be the route taken by Gwydion, King of Gwynedd, with the enchanted pigs he had stolen from Pryderi, King of Dyfed. Pryderi gave chase, following Gwydion along the stream, until there was a battle in Gwynedd which ended with the former's death.

THE CHURCH OF LLANFIHANGEL GENAU'R GLYN

A church was being built at Glanfraed, though every morning the builders awoke to discover the previous day's work had been demolished. This went on day after day until a voice was heard saying, 'Glanfraed fawr is to be herein, Llanfihangel at Genau'r Glyn.' So they built the church on the opposite side of the valley at Genau'r Glyn, where the land is so steep that coffins were buried vertically and any bones that were exposed after heavy rain were hastily reburied. The churchyard is one of the most beautiful in the county, containing a 2,000 year-old yew tree, a healing well that cured a crippled girl from Glamorgan, and the corpse of the stationmaster's son, who died aged 16 when he fell beneath the wheels of a train. A farmhouse was built at Glanfraed, which was the birthplace of the naturalist, historian and writer Edward Llwyd.

ST DAVID AND THE NIGHTINGALE

St David came to preach at the church in Llanddewi Brefi, and despite being raised up on a mound of earth, the congregation were distracted by the sweet song of a nightingale. The saint rebuked his flock for not paying attention, and ordered that the nightingale should never sing in the valley again.

THE CHAPEL ON MILL STREET

The first Methodist Chapel in Aberystwyth was built on Mill Street in 1785, and was known as Capel y Groes, the Chapel of the Cross. Such was the sweep of Methodism that the chapel was continually rebuilt to accommodate bigger congregations, and by 1880 there were four storeys and 200 people. In 2002 the chapel closed and a developer submitted plans to turn the Grade II listed building into flats, but permission was refused. In 2008 it was the only listed building in the way of a proposed development of supermarkets and car parks, and shortly after planning permission was refused it burned to the ground and the remains were demolished. Tongues began to wag that a developer had paid a tramp £5 to set fire to the chapel and keep his mouth shut. The statue of a 6ft bronze angel which stood there as a war memorial was moved to Ceredigion Museum and chained to a pillar. Plans are still afoot to develop the site, and the angel is awaiting interview.

THE LEFT LEG OF HENRY HUGHES COOPER

In Strata Florida Abbey there is a gravestone with the carving of a leg and the inscription, 'The left leg and part of the Thigh of Henry Hughes Cooper was cut off & interrd here June 18th 1756'. Henry's leg had to be amputated to save his life, but as no doctor could be found, the local butcher was called for. Henry survived and with one foot in the grave, he left for America. He planned to rejoin his leg when his time came, though the two were never reunited.

There are two graves close to Henry's, one of a tramp found burned just up the valley, the other belonging to the poet Dafydd ap Gwilym. He was born in Penrhyncoch at the beginning of the fourteenth century and was a romantic figure, said to be able to charm the nightingales into telling him their secrets. He was reputedly dating twenty women unbeknownst to each other and arranged to meet them all at the same time under the same tree while he hid in the top branches to watch the fun below.

While visiting Strata Florida, Lizzie Morgan from Mynydd Bach put her ear to a flagstone and exclaimed that she could hear the sea. She then sniffed the floor and said she could smell the sea; proof that there was a tunnel running all the way down to Monk's Cave on the coast near Llanrhystud.

PHILIP WYDDYL THE IRISHMAN

On Penrhiw there is a mound in the shape of a headless body, 4ft high with arms and legs spread out. This is reputedly the last resting place of Philip the Irishman, who lived in the church tower at Llanwenog. He was leader of a gang of thieves, and when the locals came for him, he leapt from the tower, broke his leg, was stoned to death and buried as he was when he hit the ground.

HENLLAN AND THE ITALIAN POWS

In the early 1940s a prisoner of war camp was built near the village of Henllan, and three years later around 1,500 Italian POWs lived there. Many were sent out to work on the nearby farms to replace the local men who were in the army. However, they were Catholics in a land of chapel, so in 1944 they began to build a church inside a bare Nissen hut. From the outside it looked no different to the rest of the camp, but inside it was the Church of the Sacred Heart. They made an altar from concrete and wood, a pulpit from Red Cross boxes, and pillars and candlesticks from tins of bully beef. One of the prisoners, Mario Ferlito, mixed paints from fruit and vegetables, fish bones, red cabbage, pickling juice and tea leaves, and other pigments smuggled into the camp. He painted frescos and murals on the roof and beams, including a copy of *The Last Supper* above the altar, and peepshow pictures on old roof tiles of girls in underwear climbing fences.

24

THE BRWCSOD
OF FFAIR RHOS

In the hills of north Ceredigion, they used to say that if you looked into a hole in the ground there'd be a Cornish tin miner at the bottom looking back at you. The Cornishmen had long worked in the lead mines, bringing with them lawyers and teachers, and stories of Tommy Knockers or *coblynau*, the mischievous long-limbed goblins who lived in the tunnels. They guided the miners to the best seams of ore, warned them of fire, gas, rockfall, or drove them mad with echoes of rushing water or shifting earth. Whistle or swear at the Tommy Knockers and you'd be in trouble, but never so much as glance at the Cornishmen. The children in Ffair Rhos, on the moors near Strata Florida, called them the *Brwcsod*, after the first Cornishman to come to the moor, a man by the name of Brooks. Children were taught to be fearful of the *Brwcsod*, as they were of tramps or Gypsies or any outsiders.

There was a small girl at Ffair Rhos, a dark girl with a red ribbon in her hair and round spectacles held together with tape that magnified her eyes and helped her outstare anyone who looked at her. She caught starlings to bake in pies, and her mother told her stories of the *Brwcsod*, not to go near them, to say nothing, and most of all, not to look them in the eye. But this was a girl who rarely did what she was told. She was inquisitive. She loved to watch.

It was fair day, and the girl was there, wide-eyed, polishing the lenses of her spectacles with her skirt. It was always fair day on the moor, from the first fair in spring to the May fair, the Midsummer fair, the Rood Fair and the little autumn fair. The old folk said that back in the fourteenth century, the monks from Strata Florida Abbey used to meet at the fair to buy and sell stock and wool. Now, it was the drovers who herded their cattle to Llidiart y Ffair, and business was conducted with a nod and a wink and a look over the shoulder in case anyone was watching. The fairs were places for fighting, robberies, drunkenness; unsafe for a drover, never mind a small girl. Every Rood Fair the men of Tregaron fought the men of Bont in Cross Inn Square. Twm y gof, the blacksmith from Bont, was known for beating people and maiming horses, before he was murdered in 1821 by two former associates in crime who were later hanged and delivered to surgeons to be dissected and anatomised. High on the Elenydd Moor, just over the border in Brecon, is Nantybeddau or the Valley of the Graves, a forbidding place where the *Brwcsod* robbed the drovers as they were walking home towards Rhaeadr with money stuffed in their back pockets. There were ancient gravestones, flooded when the Claerwen reservoir was built. Evan Nantybeddau rescued one and kept it at his farmhouse.

Amidst all the haggling and noise, the girl spotted the *Brwcsod*. There were three of them, dressed in dark jackets, grey woollen collarless shirts and caps pulled down over their eyes, and they were watching a drover counting out the money he had received for three fine black oxen. He set off along the road with his money, and the *Brwcsod* were away in the blink of a crow's eye. The girl followed them. They left the winding road, taking a shortcut through the dips and mounds around the Teifi Pools, until they were ahead of the drover. They hid themselves by the old mine workings at Esgair-Mwyn, and she hid herself behind an old hawthorn on the hillside. As the drover passed the mine the three men jumped him; there was a scuffle and the man was lying twisted on the ground. The girl's heart was in her mouth but she couldn't stop staring. The *Brwcsod* threw the man down a hole and filled it in with stones and rubble from the mine, then scanned the hills in case anyone had seen them. The girl melted herself into the hawthorn, pleading with it for protection, her heart beating as loudly as the knockers in the mine shaft. The men stared at the tree, and then set off towards Pontrhydfendigaid.

She stayed there, her body pressed into the bark, frozen to the spot and fearful that the *Brwcsod* were climbing up the other side of the hill to feed her to the crows. She took off her spectacles. Without her glasses, no one could see her. She tore the bright red ribbon from her hair, and dropped it to the ground. Darkness fell, fear and cold overwhelmed her, and she ran, faster than any hare or dog had ever run, heart pumping in her chest, she ran until she reached her home, threw herself on her bed and hid under the covers. She said nothing; she was terrified, but she was a strong girl, and the inquisitive streak in her drew her back to the mine, though her mind told her to tell her mother. When she reached the old hawthorn tree, there was the red ribbon from her hair, tied neatly around one of the branches in a bow.

She never saw the *Brwcsod* again. They were always moving from mine to mine, wherever there was work. No one made a fuss about the drover, as drovers were always going missing and the locals knew it was better to face the wall than face the *Brwcsod*. The fairs moved to Bont in the hope of ending the lawlessness, and the little girl never wore a red ribbon in her hair again.

THE BLACK OX BANK

As the drovers herded their cattle and sheep to the bustling livestock market at Smithfield in London, they lived in fear of robbery and their lives. For safety, they travelled in numbers, often accompanied by young girls who were looking for work as gardeners or maidservants in the houses of the rich. In 1799 the drover David Jones set up a bank, first in Llandovery, then in Lampeter and Llandeilo. It was known as Banc yr Eidion Du, the Black Ox Bank, and printed its own bank notes with a Welsh black bull on each. They were only issued to the drovers and were only redeemable at the three banks, so if a stranger walked in laden with Black Ox notes, they would be arrested as a robber, as the drovers carried little worth stealing. A few years later John Evans of Penygraig helped set up Banc y Dafad Ddu (the Black Sheep Bank) in Aberystwyth and Tregaron, with a black sheep on its banknotes. By 1811 it was in liquidation, but the Black Ox Bank thrived. David Jones died a rich man in 1839, while the bank continued until 1909, when it was bought by Lloyds, so becoming the Black Horse Bank.

THE HANGED MAN OF DYLIFE

> Life is a place, where we dig in a hole, to earn enough money, to buy enough bread, to get enough strength, to dig in a hole.

Siôn y gof, John Jones the blacksmith, lived in a cottage in Ystumtuen near Ponterwyd with his wife Catherine and their two children, Thomas and Avarina. He earned a living shoeing horses and forging metals for the local lead mines, but times were hard and work was scarce, so Siôn set off in search of work in another mine. In Ceredigion, the tradition was that a miner took a wife only when she was with child, and only for as long as he was at the mine. When he left, he also left behind his wife and children. She was like a shovel or a pit pony; the property of the mine, not the man.

Siôn left Ystumtuen alone in late 1719 and came to Dylife, a bustling mine where there was work for a hefty blacksmith. He took another wife, a maidservant at Llwyn y Gog, and he settled down to a new life. But the past is never left behind, and Catherine, poverty-stricken and starved of love, wanted her husband back. With her two children in hand, she tramped the drovers' road to Dylife, herds of cattle milling around her, watched by bandits and thieves. They arrived at the mine to find Siôn remarried, as the unwritten rulebook allowed. He has done nothing wrong, he said, men could divorce and remarry like this. Life would be too complicated otherwise. Catherine was distressed; there were feelings, desires. The heart had a say in this porridge pot of emotion, and there were children who were  growing up without a father. How could she look after her children without a wage? Take another man? She didn't want another man; she wanted her husband. But he had another wife now, and this wife loved him too. Siôn told her to go; Catherine refused. There was an argument. Siôn picked up an axe, stoved in her head and threw her down a mineshaft, the children after her. She and her son were dead, but Avarina was still alive, and in hunger she tried to drink from her mother's breast. Siôn's workmates asked him where his wife and children were, and he said that they had gone. All he could hear was the voice of his daughter, calling for milk, fainter and fainter, and soon he was a broken man.

In January 1720, three bodies were found at the bottom of a mineshaft; a woman, a boy and a girl. Siôn ran to Castle Rock above the River Clywedog but his workmates followed him and prevented him from jumping. He was put on trial in Welshpool and sentenced to be hanged. When asked why, he answered, 'Because of some other woman, and the Devil.' Siôn was taken to Pen y Crocbren (Gallows Hill), sat on a horse with a rope round his neck, and the horse made to walk. He was gibbeted, placed in an iron frame and hung out to rot for all to see. As a blacksmith, he had built his own gibbet. In death, Siôn found the work he had been seeking when he left Ystumtuen.

Siôn's head and gibbet were found in 1938 and he was displayed in a chemist's shop in Machynlleth, before he was taken to St Fagan's, where he is still on display, this time in a glass case, a very modern type of gibbeting. You can still see Catherine, too, as her ghost searches the old mine workings at Dylife for her husband. The pool below Castle Rock is known as Llyn Siôn y Go. Siôn, too, has been seen, climbing a ladder down the mineshaft, looking for his head.

LLYWERNOG SILVER LEAD MINE AND THE GROVELS OF TROGGLE HOLE

Long ago, tin miners moved up from Cornwall to work in the mines around Ponterwyd, where they built homes and chapels. A row of terraced houses is named Cornish Row after them, and they left a legacy of names such as Trevethan, Tyack, Tregoning and Nancarrow. Now another indigenous group are moving into Ponterwyd.

In spring 2012 an advert appeared in the *Cambrian News*, inviting applications for the jobs of resident orc and goblin at Llywernog Silver Lead Mine Museum. Soon the mine was inundated with applications from goblins, *bwca*s, bogeys, witches, indigenous fairies, role-play gamers from Penglais Woods, Neil Gaiman's twitter followers, and recovering goths. A small goblin from Aberystwyth got the job of goblin, while the other job went to an unemployed miner dressed as an orc. The mine has now been renamed the Silver Mountain Experience. There are two trails: the Miner's Trail, leading to the Giant Waterwheel, the Jigger Shed and the Gunpowder Magazine, while the other trail follows the path to Troggle Hole and Woo Hoo Wood, where the grovels dwell. Alongside the old mining machinery, there is a field of fly agaric furniture and a hillside planted with wind turbines. Submerged in the old mineshafts, renamed the Black Chasm, the miners long departed, the goblins tell theatrical tales that mix history, heritage, folklore, fiction and theatre into one bubbling cauldron.

The goblin is happy in her new job. Her friends and family have moved to Ponterwyd to be with her, along with hundreds of other orcs and goblins hopeful of employment, just as the Cornish tin miners did all those years ago. They have found comfort in their new community, safe from the ridicule of the rational world of reality TV. The economy of the area is reviving; shops sell ethnic grovel food, graphic novels, facsimile weapons, and limited edition resin maquettes hand signed by the original goblin. Cornish Row has been renamed Tolkien Terrace, and storytellers a hundred years from now will tell tales of Troggle Wood alongside Taliesin. You don't believe me? Well, it happened 200 years ago when an old folk tale was rewritten to attract tourists to Devil's Bridge.

THE TALKING TREE
OF CWMYSTWYTH

In a small cottage on the drovers' road near Cwmystwyth, lived a woman, her husband and their three children. Early in the 1800s Cwmystwyth was a wild place of bare hillsides, spoil heaps, mine buildings, and remote farms; a place where people survived. This was a time when land was being enclosed, men and money were being lost to the war with Napoleon, and bellies ached with hunger. The war, however, brought one benefit. Cwmystwyth was the gateway to the Hafod estate, where the great oaks were being felled to make warships, and transported along the road where the cottage stood. The woman had an idea. Using clean fresh spring water, she began brewing beer and selling it to passers-by. Soon she was earning a little money and her children's bellies grumbled a little less.

Her husband, however, was no good; a ne'er-do-well, jealous of his wife's success, he became miserable and morose. 'Give me beer,' he said, but she refused, saying it was to sell, and he would be stealing food from her children. He took to wandering the hillside in melancholia, and by the time the summer came, he was talking to an old twisted hawthorn tree that grew on the hill above the cottage. His wife was so busy brewing and selling her beer, she hardly noticed that her customers were laughing at the man who talked to trees.

By the autumn, he spent all his time with the tree, asking questions, locked in earnest conversation, nodding in answer, wide eyes on a vacant face, as the leaves fell around him. Customers were dwindling now; with November came the first snowfalls, and the road became impassable. Her husband said, 'Give me beer. My friend and I have much to discourse, and beer will help the conversation.' She refused, so he picked up a knife, held her by the hair and slit her throat. He ran outside to tell his friend the tree what he had done. The tree refused to speak to him, and the man became angry. He began to cut branches and the tree screamed.

Come February, the snows melted and travellers used the road once more, but they must have wished they hadn't. When they stopped at the cottage for a beer, the door was open to the freezing cold. Inside were the bodies of the woman and two of her children, the cold preserving them as if they were asleep. The third child was nowhere to be seen. The man was lying at the foot of his only friend, the tree. His throat was cut, and a knife was found entwined in one of the branches just above his frozen body. The wind gathered strength and blew through the snow-covered branches, and a voice was heard, saying, 'This is the end.' From that day, travellers swore they heard the tree wailing and lamenting, saying there must be justice. But how could they put a tree on trial? People would laugh.

In time, the cottage crumbled into the earth and the tree decayed and died, but its children are still there, dotted across the bare heathery slopes, dark and twisted, locked in conversation, talking to anyone who will listen.

THE THREE SISTERS

High on Pumlimon, where the curlews call and kites circle, live three sisters, Severn, Wye and Rheidol. Severn is handsome and organised; she rises early in the morning, bathes herself with spring water sprinkled with heather, and sets off on her trip to the sea, taking the scenic route to England, dancing a loop around Shrewsbury, under the Iron Bridge to Coalbrookdale, through Worcester and Tewkesbury, on her way to Gloucester. Wye rises next; she is pretty and flirty, tumbling her way through Radnorshire and Hereford, rattling over the stones between Builth and Hay and onto Hereford and Monmouth, until she meets her sister at Chepstow, where they kiss and go hand in hand to meet the lover they share, the sea. Rheidol is still in her dreams, dishevelled and lazy, who scorns her sisters' beauty and lets her hair run wild; by the time she rises it is late, and she hurries down to the dam at Nant y Moch, takes her child Mynach by the hand and rushes down to the sea at Aberystwyth. Here she joins her friend Ystwyth and they have a fine old time at the fair before sharing an ice cream on the seafront and a box of chips on the prom.

THE TAIL OF THE WHITE MARE

You have already heard of Siôn Cwilt, but here is another story.

Siôn was an old miser who, on his deathbed, told his wife that he was going to Heaven to build her a castle, and that she must follow him quickly and bring his money with her. A widow now, she was flattered by a handsome soldier, and told him of the miser's plan. The soldier offered to take the money to the old miser without the beautiful widow having to die. She gave him the money and he prepared to leave on his white horse. However, a boy had overheard everything, so the soldier placed a guinea in the boy's fist and told him that if anyone asked where he was, to say that he had gone to see an angel, and off he rode. The widow realised that she'd given all the miser's wealth away to a philanderer, and sent men in pursuit. They questioned the boy, and he told them that the soldier had gone to see an angel, pointing at a streak of white cloud in the sky. 'There,' said the boy, 'you can see the tail of the white mare disappearing into Heaven.' The men were God-fearing and saw no reason to doubt the lad, and that is why folk in Ceredigion call streaks of white cloud *cynffon y gaseg wen*, or 'the tail of the white mare'.

HEN GELL, THE OLD CELL

Back in the old Welsh dreamtime, Ceredigion was dotted with *cist feini*, altar tombs or burial chambers, consisting four large stones at right angles to each other and a flat one on top for a roof, like a big stone box. One *cist fein*, near Traethgwyn, was the home of Gwynestrin and it was known as Hen Gell. Nearby, at another *cist faen* at Cellglynlle near Cilglynlle farmstead, lived his friend Aeron.

Gwynestrin was at a banquet thrown in honour of two princes: Caredig, who gave his name to the county, and Caradog of the swarthy arm from Cornwall. These were violent times, and the two princes were murdered and Gwynestrin injured. He escaped and took a coracle across the Ystwyth where he stayed with friends until his shattered sanity and broken body recovered. He returned to Hen Gell, where he lived in voluntary imprisonment for the rest of his life, teaching, healing and imparting wisdom to the poor, the uneducated, and to anyone who wished to listen. He was known as the man in the cell.

Hen Gell disappeared in one of Ceredigion's many floods, although some old folk in the late 1800s remembered seeing the top stone above the waters. Today the name Hengell applies to a housing estate and a caravan park; all that remains to remind us that people lived in voluntary solitude, celibacy and self-imposed punishment.

THE STALLION'S BACK AND THE HEADLESS HORSE

Long ago, there was a chestnut stallion who took messages from the King of Gwynedd to Arthur in Cornwall. The stallion gripped the messages between his teeth, leapt mountains at a single bound and flew over rivers and lakes without so much as getting his hooves wet. One day, the stallion was carrying an important message and galloping so quickly that while crossing the little River Guto at Cwm Neuadd, Gilfachrheda, he dropped down dead, although

he was travelling so fast that his head carried on moving until it reached the Gower, where it dropped to the ground at Pen Mark, or the Stallion's Head. If you look at Cwm Neuadd you can see the shape of the horse, and the spot is known as Cefn March (the Stallion's Back).

Conjurers and wise women have special powers with horses, and there was a horse whisperer at Strata Florida only a few years ago. In Llanilar in 1982, during the demolition of a house, five horses' skulls – four workhorses and a pony – were found buried inside a wall. The skulls were reburied beneath the floor of the new building to offer good fortune and protection. Y Fari Lwyd, or Grey Mary, a decorated horse's skull carried around on a pole, was described as visiting houses in New Quay in 1886, walking from Siop Bili Twm at Bristol House through Tin Pan Alley to Manchester House. Y Ceffyl Pren, the wooden horse, was an old form of folk justice when an effigy of an offender would be tied to a wooden frame and marched round the village or town to the accompaniment of the clattering of pots and pans. A *ceffyl-dwr*, a water horse, followed a butter dealer home from Cardigan. In the form of a creature between man and goat, it crushed him, leaving 'great black bruises' that were seen for weeks.

THE LEGEND OF LLAN INA

Many hundreds of years ago, in a cottage at Traethgwyn where the River Llethi flows into Cardigan Bay, there lived an old couple named Gronw and Malen, with their daughter Madlen. One warm heavy day in August, dark clouds gathered and thunder and lightning struck. The family were locking in their pigs and chickens when they saw a large ship out to sea, rolling with the waves, its mast broken by a lightning strike. Gronw knew that all on board would die unless someone rescued them, but he also saw the ship was flying a Saxon flag, and he had no love for the Saxons. His heart ruled his head, and he set sail in his small rowing boat, his daughter Madlen by his side, into the teeth of the violent storm and the mouth of the raging sea. They reached the great ship as it sank in a whirlpool of brimstone, heaved seven men on board and took them to their cottage, then returned to save five more, as two others swam for the shore.

At the cottage, Malen gave the shivering men food and drink and sat them by a flaming fire. Gronw did not speak their language, but it was clear that a tall thin man dressed in fine clothes was their spokesman. He went to fetch a monk from the church at Henfynyw who could speak Anglo Saxon as well as Welsh, and after a brief conversation, the monk introduced the tall thin man as Ina, a king from England.

King Ina, in gratitude, built a church on the spot where he had been rescued, and ensured that Gronw and his family were never in want for the remainder of their days. Ina's church was engulfed in a flood many years later, but another church was built on the new shoreline, close to where the Llethi joins the sea. Llan Ina church still stands to this day.

Some say, though, that Ina and his men were saved by mermaids.

THE DRIBBLING COW
AND OTHER CURIOUS CATTLE

SIÔN AND SIÂN AND THE DRIBBLING COW

In a peeling yellow limewashed farmhouse near Fron-y-Fran lived an old couple, Siôn and Siân, and they were the original Mister and Missus, long before S4C thought of the idea. Siôn was one of those big blokes who always wore a cap, with a mask of a face that gave away little, twinkling eyes and a thin mouth with a permanent smile.

Siân, well she was small and everything irritated her; she would boil like pea soup, she would have whims, and she nagged Siôn until she got what she wanted. Get me a bonnet, a milking pail, a wicker basket, a flat iron, an enchanted pig. Now she had a whim for a little red cow to graze the steep hill at the back of the farmhouse for her. So Siôn let her boil and then he bought one for her. £4 5s it cost, although he had bought not a red one, but a black one. Siân was angry with Siôn because she only wanted a red cow; red and white would have done, but not black. 'Take it back. Don't want it,' she said. But black it was, and black it stayed.

She stopped speaking and sulked. She took her lunch of swede and potato mashed in a basin with butter, and she chewed each mouthful slowly, and while she ate she stared at the cow. And there she was and there was the cow. And the cow chewed her cud and stared back at Siân, and the cow dribbled from her mouth. And only the Devil knows why, but Siân saw red and thought the cow was laughing at her for dribbling while she was chewing her mash, so she took a hammer, hit it between the horns and killed it, stone dead, without a peep. When she saw what she'd done, she came to her senses and dropped dead of shock, right there on the spot. When Siôn came home from his day in the fields, he found the corpses of Siân and the cow lying there. He said nothing, he just stared with the smile he couldn't remove, and then he died of shock too. And there's an end to the story for you.

THE THREE ROAN CALVES

Once there were two farmers: one rich and bald, one poor and hairy. The rich farmer had three sons, Twm, Siôn and Dai, and the poor farmer had one daughter, Beti. Oh, she was pretty. She had eyes as blue as the sea, lips as red as the roses that grew round the door, and hair as yellow as ripe wheat. But don't take my word. All three boys were heart over head in love with her, and each of them asked their father for a fat dowry so they could marry her. Well, there was a problem: which boy to choose? The rich farmer scratched his bald head and decided to give each son a roan calf, and whoever got the best price at Lampeter Fair would marry Beti. The poor farmer agreed, for this would mean he would be poor no more. Beti, it seems, had no say in the matter.

If truth be told, Twm, the eldest, was a lazy boy – a good-for-nothing, a wastral, a loafer, but he wanted to marry the girl because it was easier than courting. Dai was a womaniser, he was mean and he cared little for the girl, but wanted to marry her because there might be money in it. Siôn, well, he wasn't a good looker, but he was clever, could charm the birds and he believed in true love. So the boys were given their roan calves, and soon Twm's was ailing because he couldn't be bothered to feed it, Dai's was looking well, but Siôn's was better.

Would you believe it, Siôn and Beti were courting in secret under an old yew tree in the churchyard, and no one ever disturbed them because nobody knew. One night by the light of the moon, Siôn was waiting for Beti when he spotted Dai in the churchyard, cutting branches from a yew tree. Not long after this, Siôn's calf died. He couldn't understand why when it had been growing so well, until he found a yew branch by its trough. Then he knew. Dai had added the yew, which is poison to horned beasts, to the feeding trough to kill Siôn's calf. So what did Siôn do? Well he skinned the calf and he waited.

Come Lampeter Fair, Twm had a shabby old calf that no one wanted to buy, Dai had a beautiful roan calf, and Siôn had no calf at all. Dai sold his calf for £3, and set off home to claim Beti's hand, the farm and her dowry. Siôn was having fun at the fair, where there was a raggedy old tinker dressed in a rabbit-skin hat with ear flaps, a patchwork suit, clogs on his feet, a white woolly beard that came down to his waistcoat, a sack round his neck and leather shoelaces hanging from a pole. He was singing 'Rhic, rhocs, ceirion, clocs' over and over. People were buying the leather shoelaces, tuppence a go, and he was selling hundreds because they were made from the finest leather, and he placed the money in the sack. All the children were following him singing 'Rhic, rhocs, ceirion, clocs' and everyone was dancing with the old tinker. At the end of the fair, the old tinker's back was bent with the weight of his sack, and after he sold the last pair of shoelaces he vanished as quietly as a cat.

Back at the farm, Dai was counting out £3 in front of the two farmers, and claimed Beti as his wife. Before anything was agreed, there was a knock at the door. Beti opened it and in walked the raggedy old tinker from the fair, looking like a tramp. He asked for lodgings for the night, and the rich farmer agreed in return for whatever money he may have, so the tinker tipped out the money he had made selling shoelaces. It was all pennies and tuppences, so the old farmer asked Beti to count it all. While she was doing this, the old tinker pulled off his beard and his shabby clothes and who should be standing there but Siôn himself. Siôn explained that he had made the money from selling leather shoelaces he had made from his little roan calf, so if he had made more money than Dai, then the girl should be his. The money was counted and it came to £3 5s. Siôn had won, Beti was delighted, Dai was found out, and Twm, well, he was probably sleeping off the drink in the barn with the chickens.

THE YCHEN BANNOG

Two long-horned oxen, the Ychen Bannog, were pulling a heavy stone over the mountain to help build the church at Llanddewi Brefi, leaving a deep furrow behind them. There was a great rock in their path, and in their efforts to pull their load over the rock, one of the oxen let out a great bellow and died. It is said the Ychen Bannog are bound together and one cannot live without the other. Such was the pain of the remaining ox that it bellowed nine times, and the sound split the rock in two. The ox pulled the stone on its own to the church, before it too died. There is a deep furrow stretching from the Llanddewi Brefi to Strata Florida, known to this day as Cwys yr Ychen Bannog.

A horn from one of the Ychen Bannog was kept in the church, where it stayed until 1953 when it was moved to the Welsh Folk Museum at St Fagans. Tests revealed that it belonged to a 2,000-year-old long-horned wild cow. The white wild cattle at Dinefwr are said to be their descendants, although they are small and creamy white, far more like fairy cattle.

THE FAIRY CATTLE OF LLYN EIDDWEN

On the highest hills of Mynydd Bach, above Trefenter, where a woman named Lizzie once encountered a magic calf, lie the three lakes of Eiddwen, Fanod and Farch. Of Farch is told the simple but poignant story that a most wonderful animal came out of the lake, only to be shot by a local farmer. Farch is now dry, and it is said that when Eiddwen dries up, Carmarthen will sink.

Fairy cattle live in both Fanod and Eiddwen. They can be seen at twilight on moonlit evenings, grazing on the meadowsweet and soft rushes that grow round the edge of the lakes, fleeing back into the waters at the sight of people. They are creamy white with long horns and once gave the finest frothiest creamiest milk, keeping the locals in cream and cheese. A few years ago, a writer from

Mynydd Bach drove past the lake on her way to view the house she was thinking of moving into, saw a herd of cattle paddling by the water's margins, and knew this was the place where she was to live. In 2012, the same woman found a stork standing on her doorstep. She was surprised as storks rarely appear in Britain, and wondered if she was about to have another child. In the morning the bird left, but was verified by the British Trust for Ornithology as a stork. Shortly after, a friend of the woman's in nearby Llangwyryfon, who was overdue, gave birth to a baby boy.

A CEREDIGION MATADOR

The journalist Gareth Jones, former aide to Lloyd George and the man who exposed Stalin's role in the Russian famine in the early 1930s, wrote of an encounter with a matador near East Gwaun-cae-Gurwen Colliery. He was a short, wiry Cardi, with flushed cheeks, who had come to a farm, Bryn Awel, for his health. He told Mr Jones calmly of his fight with a bull upon the mountain. The bull came rushing full speed towards him but the little man stood his ground until the beast was almost upon him then, with his stick, he struck it a crashing blow over the eyes. He was quite unconcerned at the struggle. 'Were you not terrified?' Jones asked. The Cardi was surprised at his question. 'Oh, I'm quite used to it in Cardiganshire,' he replied.

THE ELEPHANT
THAT DIED IN TREGARON

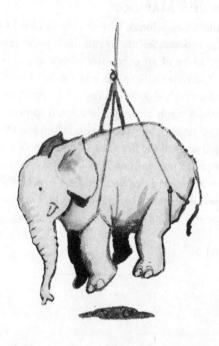

In 1784, Phlip Astley, cavalryman and horse trainer, built an equestrian amphitheatre on the South Bank of the Thames in London to promote shows of rare horsemanship. Astley's Amphitheatre was wooden constructed, and was destroyed four times by fire and reconstructed until it was rebuilt for the final time in 1841 by William Batty, showman and purveyor of animal circuses, camel and ostrich races, tumblers and acrobats, the juggler of Antwerp, the Devil Rider, and the German Voltigeur. There were a whole family of Battys, all of them from circus stock, artistes and fairground folk. Lena the equestrienne, Thomas the lion tamer (scarred by a tiger), Madame Frederica and her amazing performing dog, and the hero of our tale, George Batty, with his Travelling Menagerie of Indian and African leopards, crested porcupines, a magnificent specimen of the drill baboon, a young Russian bear, a pair of Irish badgers, a handsome blue macaw (very rare), and 'Rajah', a 7 year-old Indian elephant who was very docile and trained to carry children. Animals were captured in nets, transported by ship, winched ashore and kept in cages. These are practices that sit unkindly with us now, but this was a different world: a world we wouldn't survive in; the harsh world of fairy tale. George had watched William's business burn to the ground four times, and he was a smart man who knew that there was a whole world outside London, full of punters anxious to see his animals. The answer was not to keep rebuilding the amphitheatre, but to take to the road.

On a Sunday in May 1848, Batty's Travelling Menagerie pulled into the village square of Tregaron, on its way to the fairs at Aberystwyth and Cardigan. It was raining old women with sticks as the wagons formed a circle outside the Talbot Hotel, the old drover's inn. This was a very different world to the one they knew; where farmers drove cattle and sheep rather than elephants. In London they'd be pouring in, rowdy and rumbustious, the language blue, anxious to see the exotic, but here they just stared. It was hard to know if they were excited, interested or just miserable. George was confused. He was a simple man who believed in plain speaking. They should say what they mean. Couldn't they speak the Queen's English? And the tea they drank was as weak as ditchwater. Tregaron tea. He was approached by a preacher, a stern chapel man who railed against him, not for the cruelty he was showing to his animals or the cages in which he had incarcerated them, but for daring to move his menagerie on a Sunday when their thoughts should be with God. An altercation ensued. They disagreed, the preacher strode away shaking his head in need of prayer, and George repaired to the Talbot, in need of whisky. And here's the point in our story where the truth of history merges with the truth of folk tale.

There was a boy, sat on a wooden bench beneath the front window of the public bar, gazing at the caravans and creatures in the square, staring as only shaggy dark-haired boys can. He was smart and simple; the girls liked to stroke him. He shuffled up to George who was sitting on his own in the corner of the bar, trying to dry his rain-soaked clothes, shunned by the men in the snug who were speaking a language he didn't understand. 'Mr Elephant Man?'

'Whatcha want, guttersnipe?'

'Your elephant is sick. I can help him,' said the boy, with a big smile from ear to ear. 'What do you know about elephants, street urchin?' asked George. The boy explained, 'I know an elephant named Maharajah refused to get on a train and walked from Edinburgh to Belle Vue Zoo in Manchester, where it lived in misery. I know it took 152 bullets to kill one named Chunee who had killed his cruel keeper. My nan knows all about them, I've ridden them in my dreams, and I know your elephant is sick.' Batty laughed dismissively and threw the boy a coin. 'Ere, clever dick. Take my elephant to the stables of the hotel, bed him down in straw and water him. We're out o' this God forsaken' hole tomorrow.' The boy ran outside, took the elephant by its rope, whispered in its ear, led it to the stable and bedded it down. The animal was agitated, distressed, in pain. The boy stared at it with deep green eyes, whispered in its ear, and it calmed a little.

He poured spring water over the elephant to cool its temperature, and ran off to see his nan. She lived alone in a remote cottage in the hills where no one visited, except the afflicted and those seeking cures or a cup of herbal tea. There was nothing she didn't have a herb for, and no question she couldn't answer. She could curse and she could lift the curses of others. She could fly and enter the minds of wild animals, living with them in the woods while her body lay abed. She had bottles of tinctures in a cabinet with a creaky door, and a cauldron boiling on the hearth, spitting green liquid onto the flagstone floor where it sizzled. She could charm the birds from the sky; she could do anything but go to chapel. She said that there was a cure for everything but rain and preachers. The boy told her about the elephant and Mr Batty and the stable, and she became all of a flutter, gathering bottles and phials and powders into a bag, talking to herself and disturbing the spiders in their webs.

When the boy and his Nan arrived at the stable, the elephant was convulsing, sweating and thrashing from side to side, ridden with agues, fevers and colics. 'He's hallucinating, poor dear,' said Nan. There was no time to waste. She tried every potion, every incantation; to the old woman it was deadly serious, but the boy found it rather comical. The fever didn't relent. 'I'll have to go in.' said the old lady. 'What do you mean, Nan?' asked the boy.

'I can't mend the poor creature from out here. He's too much of a big one. I must meet him inside. Promise me you will carry my body home and place it in my old rocker by the hearth. Keep it warm and keep the world away. I'll be back when my work is done.' With that Nan began to shake and loosen her limbs, first slowly and then frantically. Freeing her body from her mind, she gibbered incoherently and went into a trance, just like the old soothsayers that Giraldus met over 800 years before. Her movements reached

a frenzy and her body crumpled; the boy caught her, and her mind went inside the great grey body. It was as dense as the dark woods in there, but she knew what she must do. She slowed its heartbeat until there was barely a sound.

Back in the stable, the elephant had calmed and hardly moved. The boy carried his nan's frail body home and placed her in the old mahogany rocking chair, stoked up the fire and wrapped a shawl around her shoulders. He had seen this before, but never with such a great creature; only with horses and cattle. In the morning, Batty went to the stable and found the elephant sat upright, limp and cold, for all the world as if it were dead. 'Curse this place. Too many preachers and too much lead in the water.' He went outside and ordered the wagons to roll. In the early hours of Monday morning, Batty's Travelling Menagerie trundled away from Tregaron, unaware that it had created a whole new folktale, a potential tourist industry and a great Welsh myth.

The townsfolk were bemused by the elephant, but they felt compassion for the poor creature and did their best to care for it. They kept it warm and brought it water, and one small boy was often seen whispering in its ear and staring into its eyes, though it barely breathed. The townsfolk wrote to the local newspaper declaring how concerned they were for the suffering of this strange animal so alien to their culture, as did the preacher who had argued with Batty, declaring how offended he was by the menagerie owner's ignorance of the Sabbath. Some said that it had drunk water contaminated with waste from the mines in the hills and was dying of lead poisoning.

A week later, it had vanished, and the mystery began. Folk memory tells that it died and was buried at the back of the Talbot Hotel, or maybe dragged over the mountain; either way, it would have been a great effort. But two people knew the truth, and they also knew that no one would believe them. Late that night, old Nan's mind left the elephant and returned to her body, and no one saw the boy leading the groggy elephant down the main street towards Pontrhyfendigaid, out of the town to the remote cottage in the hills where the townsfolk never set foot. The old woman's mind often paid a visit to the elephant, the boy had the finest playmate a child could ever ask for, and it lived on home-made *bara brith* buns for the rest of its natural life.

You seem a little sceptical, my friend. What if I tell you there was an elephant living on a farm near Lampeter a few years ago? You could occasionally see it from the X40 bus on its way to Carmarthen. A recent archaeological dig at the back of the Talbot, organised by University of Wales Trinity Saint David, failed to find the elephant, to the amusement of those who said it was under the car park or had been dumped over the hill. And let's not forget that elephants were not uncommon in mid-Wales. Menageries and circuses visited regularly, and elephants were more than simply paintings on the Jumbo Circus Attraction at Studt's November Fun Fair in Cardigan, or the famous photo in Ceredigion museum of Salt and Pepper from Wombwell's Menagerie bathing in the sea off North Beach, Aberystwyth in 1911. There is a child's drawing of the elephant hanging in the Talbot and everyone has an opinion of where they think it is. There is another theory, postulated by a mischievous man of the neighbourhood, that poverty and hunger drove the locals to make a spectacularly large cauldron of *cawl* that fed the town all summer long.

THE WICKED FOLK OF TREGARON

The folk of Tregaron once had the reputation of being particularly wicked. They spent their time in grotesque feasting and hideous orgies. They had been warned on many occasions that if they did not cease their wickedness, their town would be destroyed by fire and flood, though they were so wicked that this only encouraged them to indulge themselves even more. One night, when their revelry was reaching its peak, storm clouds gathered, a crash of thunder was heard and a fork of lightning set fire to a tree. It rained old ladies with sticks, and floodwaters engulfed the town. Those who were not burned were drowned, and not a soul survived.

THE QUEER OLD COUPLE
WHO ALWAYS QUARRELLED

In an old cottage near Llanafan, close by the river Ystwyth, all rising damp and yellow limewash, lived the queer old couple who always quarrelled. They argued over everything: how many spare pennies were in the jar behind the clock, how many stitches were needed in the patchwork quilt, how many grains of salt they should add to the stew. Every argument always finished the same way, with the old woman going down to the river, climbing onto the overhanging branch of an old oak tree, and threatening to drown herself unless her husband admitted he was in the wrong. He always climbed down, and then so did she.

It had always been like this, ever since they were young and passionate, and he came home and found that the two pot dogs on the windowsill were facing away from each other. Every home had two ceramic pot dogs that were kept on the mantelpiece or the front window ledge. They always faced each other, but if one was turned to look away, it was a sign from the woman of the house to the gentlemen of the neighbourhood that her husband was out. From that day on, they argued about everything. From the bickering and biting, love grew.

One day, they were arguing over how many fleas the cat had when the old man walked out, took an axe and almost – but not quite – chopped through the tree branch. He went back to the cottage, and continued the argument. The old woman stormed out, climbed the tree, and perched on the end of the branch, threatening to drown herself. The branch broke and in she fell. He refused to pull her out until she admitted she was in the wrong.

Cardi Joke

Ceredigion is famous for laughing at itself.

An old farmer had to go into hospital for an operation. As soon as he arrived, he was given a good bath. As he was being dried he said to the nurse, 'Well, I'm glad that's over. I've been dreading that operation for years.'

The Old Miser, or the Man Who Gave Away Money

In folk tales, Cardis are well known for looking after their pennies (perhaps not surprisingly, as there have never been many pennies in the county, and folk were frequently forced to eat starling meat or the straw from their mattresses). However, some years ago there was an old miser from Cardigan who was thought to be the richest man in Ceredigion. He collected scrap and knick-knacks, and haggled over everything. He'd have sold his grandmother if she'd been alive. He even sold the time of day. He used the same teabag for a week. Tregaron tea, they called it.

But in his wealth he was unhappy; he was scared of being robbed. One day he was walking by the Teifi when he met a rich man. He asked the man how he came by his wealth and why he looked so happy. The man explained that he had stood on the bridge over the Dyfi at Machynlleth between Montgomeryshire and Merionethshire with a bag of gold sovereigns and offered to give them away. The old Cardi was horrified. 'What, give away money? What a silly idea.' The rich man explained that no one took him up on the offer, but they were so amused by his silliness that they thought they could do the same. So they stood on the bridge and offered sovereigns, and the rich man helped himself to a single coin from each person, and staggered away under the weight of the gold. He did the same on bridges in Caernarfon, Carmarthen, Montgomery, Pembroke, and Brecon, and soon he had more wealth than he needed. The old miser was impressed and decided to try the joke in Ceredigion.

He took a bag of gold sovereigns, and stood on the bridge over the Teifi in Cardigan. He offered a coin to everyone who walked past, certain they would find it so comical they would give their wealth to him. But Cardis are not like other folk, and soon his bag was empty and they stood by the castle walls laughing like drains at the man who was silly enough to offer them money and think they'd say no.

Cardi Joke

'Has that old Cardi farmer paid his bill yet?' asked the dentist's wife. 'No', replied the dentist, 'he not only refused, he gnashed my own teeth at me.'

Siani-pob-man

Jane Leonard was born in 1834 at Bannau Duon Farm in Llanarth to a farming family. Her mother never married and stories tell that she lived amongst the Gypsies, fled the workhouse with her brother, and that she was poorly treated in love. Shortly after her mother's death in 1883, she left her home in Aberaeron and went to live in a ramshackle clom cottage on the beach at Cae Bach, in the rent-free no man's land between the tide line and the cliff. It was so dilapidated that she stuffed the holes in the walls with rags and used old sacking to cover the windows, while smoke from her fire steamed through the gaps in the thinly thatched roof. The sea often came in through the front door at high tide, so she took shelter upstairs with her chickens, Bidi, Kit, Ruth and Charlotte, Ledi and Cynddylan, who laid their eggs in her bed, and Jonathan the cockerel. She wandered through New Quay selling white eggs dyed with strong tea to make them a more attractive brown. No one liked them as her hens lived on scraps from the beach which made the eggs taste of seaweed. Folk called her Siani'r Ieir or Siani of the eggs, though most knew her as Siani-pob-man, Jane Everywhere.

She smoked a pipe, wore clogs on her feet, a black dress with red stripes, a red and white patterned shawl, and a battered trilby hat held in place by a red and yellow handkerchief tied over her head. She posed for tourists in front of her home and sold postcards of herself. On the back of one was printed, 'Siani-pob-man does her bit to keep the Cei famous, whilst others do nothing but live on

the back of her notoriety.' She charged tourists a penny to tell their fortunes, and if anyone laughed she threw stones at them. She held court outside her cottage, singing songs and telling tales, and was very popular with visiting miners from South Wales. For a piece of tobacco, she would sing her favourite hymn, 'Ar fôr tymhestlog teithio 'rwyf'. The locals loved her; poems were written about her, she was given food parcels and supported by the Poor Law. When she died in 1917, they found £120 in a box under her bed, which she had left to the infirmary at the local workhouse. She was buried with her mother at Henfynwy, one wall of her cottage is still visible beneath the cliff, and her memory lingers long in the minds of those who never knew her.

CARDI JOKE

There was a Ceredigion farmer who stuck a mirror to his dog's feeding bowl to fool him into thinking he was getting two bones.

JOHN HARRIES, THE LITTLE TAILOR OF DIHEWYD

John was born in 1815 and grew to be 3ft 8in tall and weighed 65lbs. He married Margaret from Henfynyw who was 5ft 5in and 195lbs, and they had nine children, all of average height. They produced postcards of themselves which they used as business cards or sold at the fairs, and once went on a tour of Glamorgan to promote themselves. He was partial to a drink, his wife frequently carrying him home from the pub slung over her shoulder wrapped in her apron. At a fair, a drover told John to be quiet or he'd put him in his pocket, and John replied that there would then be more sense in the pocket that in the man's head. He was a proud man and always turned down offers from freak shows, such as at Llanarth fair, where two dwarves sang the song 'Sian a Siencyn', and danced after each verse. The words were printed on a sheet which was sold at the fair for a penny, so that everyone could join in the last verse with gusto. Stuffed two-headed calves were very commonly displayed in freak shows, and Ceredigion Museum has one that was born in 1938 in Rhydypennau with five legs and two tails, but died a fortnight later.

CARDI JOKE

One year a Ceredigion farmer had an exceptional crop which he contemplated gloomily and declared, 'I'm sure such a fine crop will put a terrible strain upon the land.'

GENTLEMEN OF THE ROAD

George Gibbs from Glasgow walked the road for fifty years, the last twenty around Lampeter, where he worked on farms and learned Welsh. He pushed his belongings round in a pram, often down the middle of the busy main road into Machynlleth at night. He was a friend of clergymen, politicians and policemen, and around a hundred people attended his funeral in Capel Brondeifi church-yard, and carried out his last request to be buried with his beard intact to the sound of 'Scotland the Brave' and 'Keep Right On to the End of the Road'.

Dafydd Gwallt Hir was a kindly intelligent poet and translator who lived in Ceredigion for fifty years. He had a photograph album containing pictures of himself, on the front of which he wrote in Welsh, 'The Year that Locusts Ate'. He translated songs, including ''Twas on the Isle of Capri that I met her,' and famously said 'The hardship of freedom is better than one day in captivity.'

Twm Barels roamed the countryside mending umbrellas, which he pushed around in a cart, though the umbrellas often looked worse after he had repaired them.

Pegi Mag lived in Ystumtuen, begging butter, bread, sugar and tea, which she took in exchange for a peek at her pet rat.

John Brown, known as Carnera after a boxer, rode a bicycle whilst wearing a sack with a knife between his teeth. His tombstone reads, 'Tall man born in Devonshire, Doing field work be seen no more, Helped two blades of grass to grow, Where one did show before.'

Mari Parry, second-hand dealer, pig farmer and horse dealer of Tan y Bwlch, didn't believe in banks yet was reputedly the richest woman in Aberystwyth, owning nine houses and a farm. She kept a tramp house, a room at the back of the Three Tuns, where she used to board the gentlemen of the road. She would boil their clothes for them, and each day make a big 'sospan' of *cawl* containing sheep's heads.

Joseph Jenkins, the Welsh Swagman, born in Ystrad Aeron in 1818, was a farmer in Tregaron before emigrating for a new life as a Swagman in Australia when he was 50. There he would have been forgotten, but he kept a daily diary for fifty-eight years. He worked as a street cleaner in Castlemaine, won the Ballarat Eisteddfod for thirteen consecutive years, and wrote that his diary was his own version of building his own monument.

Cardi Joke

A farm hand, when being interviewed for a new job, was asked why he left his old one. 'Well, you see, the food was bad. When the old cow died we had leathery beef for a month. When the old pig died we had rubbery pork for a month. And when the boss's mother-in-law died, I left damn quick.'

The Strongest Man in Aberystwyth

Lewis Jones, born 1869 in Llanddeiniol and brought up in Penparcau, was the strongest man in Aberystwyth. He was a stonemason, and cut all the stones during the building of the Aber promenade extension in 1901. He was partial to a drink and prone to sleeping in Llanbadarn churchyard after a night at the Llew Du, when he'd been locked out by his wife Margaret. He once hung a policeman over Trefechan Bridge by the ankles in exchange for five months in Swansea Prison. He sold an apple tree, dug it up, and sold it again, repeatedly. He also dug a trench single-handedly to float a stranded boat. He died in 1940 and still sleeps in Llanbadarn churchyard.

JULIE'S BEEN WORKING FOR THE DRUGS SQUAD

OPERATION JULIE

In the late 1960s, a gentleman of the London psychedelic scene moved to Cefn Bedd in Llanddewi Brefi bringing with him Eric Clapton, Jimi Hendrix, John Lennon, several Rolling Stones and, for six weeks in 1969, Bob Dylan. The locals were a little bemused, but not opposed to the strangers, who seemed harmless enough. They took drugs, but so did many of the locals who as young-sters traditionally sampled the little field mushrooms that grew in the meadows. A few years later, a chemist from Cambridge, Richard Kemp – along with his partner Christine Bott – also moved to Llanddewi Brefi to lead the good life. Presumably, the curious laboratory equipment was for home brew. Then Smiles Hughes and Buzz Healey moved to Tregaron, to lead an outrageously hippy lifestyle. Smiles clearly had money, as he would often buy drinks all round in the Talbot, and was rumoured to keep his cash in an old cornflake packet in a kitchen cupboard. This endeared him to the locals who traditionally mistrusted banks, preferring to stash their cash in milk churns, mattresses or behind the pot hen on the Welsh dresser.

Soon more and more strangers moved to the area and lived together in a house called Bronwydd. Were they birdwatchers attracted by the last refuge of the red kite, or a commune of friendly gay gentlemen fleeing the prying eyes and pointing fingers of metropolitan life? Two of them were women, and soon there were stories of free love and orgies. The strangers were dressed in sleeveless fur waistcoats, bell bottoms, bandanas round their heads and droopy moustaches, and were greeted by café owners and landlords with knowing smiles. This was the uplands of Ceredigion, where everyone knew everyone else's business, and the locals knew their own hippies, so could easily recognise a policeman dressed up as one.

In an attempt to infiltrate Kemp's drug ring, Chief Inspector Dick Lee from London had launched Operation Julie, and twenty-eight officers had been given a crash course on how to hold a spliff, psychedelic music from Tangerine Dream to Pink Floyd, incoherent speech, transcendental meditation, R Crumb and the art of underground comics, and how to go on a trip without leaving your bedroom. They were then released into the community to gather evidence for a drugs bust. Dick Lee and an army of detectives were spotted one morning crawling across a field on their bellies in the hope of surprise arrests. The innocent daughter of a local café owner who had been to art college found her home in Kingston-on-Thames being staked out by plain clothes policemen. Phones began to buzz and children were sent door to door with coded messages. A local constable's wife tipped off the hippies, the hippies repaid the kindness by supplying the locals, and some of the police began to turn native. One farmer was offered £10,000 to look after a holdall, Rolex watches were being given away, and £5 notes were used to light cigarettes. One of the dealers was rumoured to be a close personal friend of Princess Margaret.

On 26 February 1977, Operation Julie came to a head, with 120 arrests after raids on eighty-seven homes, and seventeen people sent to prison, including a thirteen-year sentence for Richard Kemp. Dick Lee claimed that Llanddewi Brefi was the centre of production of half the world's LSD. It transpired that Kemp had been Ronald Stark's assistant in the Brotherhood of Eternal Love and had discovered a cheap and simple method of synthesising LSD, for which Stark had taken the credit. Curiously, relatively little money was found, apart from some Swiss bank accounts, although 6 million tabs of LSD were confiscated by the police. There are stories of a stash of gold buried on a hilltop near the village, but no one has found it. Smiles Hughes was never arrested and continued to live it up in Llanddewi Brefi, where he is regarded as a legend, the mischievous grandson of Twm Siôn Cati, evading the police to supply the poor. And as The Clash blew away the hippy generation, Joe Strummer and Mick Jones wrote, 'Julie's Been Working for the Drugs Squad' after Sergeant Julie Taylor, who participated in the operation.

THE BIG BLACK SLUG OF CWMTYDU

It was 1913. Britain was about to go to war, and an old woman was walking home to Cwmtydu over Pencraig when she saw a monster in the bay. It was large and long and dark, like a cigar. She had never seen anything like it, but she'd heard stories about the Loch Ness Monster's Welsh cousin, the *afanc*. She ran down to the village and into the pub, babbling and gibbering, saying there was a big black slug out to sea and it was coming to eat them all. The men went outside, clutching their beer pots, and saw two men dressed in greatcoats and caps, rowing ashore from a German U-boat. The locals met them as they embarked and spoke to them in Welsh, and the two men replied in what sounded like broken English. Each thought the others were English and there was much gesticulation and misunderstanding, though the two men appeared to be saying they needed water from the stream. Their water containers were filled, they were shown into the pub, given a drink and a plate of *bara brith* and invited to warm themselves by the blazing hearth. The two German officers then politely thanked the landlord, returned to their U-boat and submerged, while the old woman always swore she had seen a giant slug.

German U-boats did patrol the Irish Sea, and crews were known to come ashore at night looking for fresh water to cool their batteries. During the First World War, there were stories of the Irish Republic giving them a safe haven, and in the 1940s the British Government laid thousands of mines in Cardigan Bay to protect the approaches to Milford Haven oil refinery.

The Tregaron Triangle

Ceredigion is renowned for strange lights, which have been variously interpreted as corpse candles, gas emissions from bogs, spacecraft, satellites, model aircraft, the Northern Lights, a UFO invasion, Chinese lanterns or stealth aircraft from the secret airbase at Aberporth. Between 2002 and 2012, Dyfed Powys Police reported thirty-three unidentified sightings, a third of which were in 2009. A retired vet wrote about the unusual number of sightings as 'the Dyfed Enigma,' and *Cambrian News* columnist Llowarch wrote of strange lights in 'the Tregaron Triangle' in the mid-1980s. In 1997 a pressure group sent a petition to the local MP Cynog Dafis to present to the government, inviting them to explain the plethora of UFO sightings in Cardigan Bay.

Motorists have reported seeing a Second World War bomber flying silently above the A44 at Eisteddfa Gurig towards Pumlumon, about 15–20ft off the ground. A mile from the road, by an old lead mine, is the wreckage of an old World War II Lancaster Bomber. In 2007 a man saw the Lancaster over the A470 at Cwm Llinau, Dyfi Estuary. In 2008 the *Cambrian News* printed an article referring to the Aber X-Files, inspired by American TV series *The X-Files* which had long since ended on TV, but as folk memory will tell you, Aber has always shown films and TV a little later than the rest of the country.

THE COMMANDO WHO TRIED TO BLOW UP A POET

Dylan Thomas, poet and playwright, moved to New Quay in 1944 with his wife Caitlin. They rented a small cottage named Majoda, a stone's throw from where the poet's childhood friend Vera Williams lived. Vera was a sculptress who had been apprenticed to Henry Moore, and was now married to Captain William Killick, a commando in the British Army. Dylan had been best man at the Killicks' wedding the year before, and they were great supporters of his talent. The Thomases moved to New Quay to be near Vera while William was serving in Greece, and soon net curtains began to twitch with talk about the great poet and his two ladies. When William returned he was clearly shell shocked. During a night at the Black Lion with Dylan and Caitlin, there was an altercation and William was thrown into the street. Some said it was to do with Dylan's Russian secretary; others that William was furious that the Thomases had been living on his military pay while entertaining their arty-farty friends. Some said William made an anti-Semitic remark, but Caitlin said that folk had been discussing a ménage à trois. Later that evening William returned home after drinking in a nearby pub, took a machine gun and a hand grenade and set off for Majoda. He sprayed the house with bullets and threatened to blow the poet to smithereens before he was arrested and charged with attempted murder. At the trial, William was found not guilty, and shortly after, the Thomases left New Quay.

THE SUPERMARKET HORSEBURGER

Early in 2013, traces of horsemeat were found in beefburgers in a supermarket of great renown. Some thought this could only be a folk tale, similar to the hundreds of urban legends from the 1970s

about horses' heads being found in abattoirs and pet poodles discovered at the back of restaurant freezers. However, it turned out to be true and an apology was made, but not until after several pantomime horses had been seen running round the aisles of the poor beleaguered supermarket shouting, 'Mummy, I want my Mummy.' Soon jokes were flowing: why does everyone in the supermarket have such long faces; what do you want on your burger, a fiver each way; why do burgers have such a high Shergar content. Even veggie burgers didn't escape, being suspected of containing UniQuorn. Some said why all the fuss, as they had known for donkey's years.

Rumours spread that the meat had come from an abattoir near Aberystwyth, and once again this folk tale turned out to be true. A respected local butcher placed a sign outside his shop saying, 'No horse meat here and that's straight from the horse's mouth', while an organic café apologised to its customers for the lack of horse in their products. For years, many folk in Aberystwyth had been fighting the coming of more supermarkets to the town, so it was somewhat ironic that the meat for the burgers was being produced on their doorstep.

Shortly after the scandal broke, ponies were dumped on Cefn Manmoel, a range of hills near Blackwood in Gwent. They became so emaciated by the poor quality of the grass on the mountain that their hunger left them unable to eat processed horse feed. Many died in the freezing early spring temperatures, while others were saved by the efforts of local people who fed them with hay and carrots.

THE KING OF
THE ROCKS

There was once a king from a faraway land. He lived in a white palace and his people loved him. He was a big man, dark and handsome, a gentle giant, but so painfully shy that he no longer appeared in front of his people. He preferred to stand in front of a full-length mirror like the queen from 'Snow White', wear wild clothes from a dressing-up chest, sing and dance the lonesome nights away, and dream of running away to another faraway land where no one would know who he was; a land of pavement cafés, seaside smells and artist's sketchbooks.

One day when his servants came to bring him breakfast, the king was not in his bedchamber. They searched the palace for him, but he had vanished. They waited to see if he would come home. His cook placed his dinner on the table, as she always had. Days and weeks and months passed and still he did not return, so his advisers read a proclamation to the people saying that the king was missing, presumed dead. The people wept and built shrines and left flowers and tied messages and items of clothing to the palace gates.

The king, however, was very much alive. He had slipped out of the palace in the middle of the night dressed as a hobo, taking his sketchbook and a little cash from the royal coffers. He walked the long tramping road, riding the rails and hitching lifts until he came to the coast. There he paid an old sea captain to stow away on board a tramp steamer, bound across the Great Ocean. After months at sea eating nothing but soused herring and drinking rum, he lost the spare tyre around his waist and was scarcely recognisable.

They docked in the port of Bristol, where many a slave had been brought, and after a hearty meal in a Thali café, he walked over a great bridge and into a new land. He tramped north and west until he was on a mountain road, all purple heather and yellow gorse, circling kites and bubbling curlews. He sat down to drink in the beauty of the land, breathed the cool mountain air into his lungs, and he knew in his bones that this is where he would live. He took out his paints and wrote his name in great letters on a roadside rock. He smiled at the sight of his name and thanked the land very much, then walked on until he came to the sea, to a small salty seaweedy town where 30,000 starlings danced in the air and slept under the pier, while the tramps danced on the prom and slept in the night shelters.

He took lodgings with an elderly spinster near the cliff railway. She, too, loved to dance and sing, hidden from prying eyes, and each evening she played 78s on her gramophone and she and the king jived the hours away to Stuff Smith and Bix Beiderbecke. Soon he felt that he would live here until the end of his days. Then his money ran out, so he took a job in a fish and chip emporium on a side street just off the promenade. It was run by an old fisherman, Islwyn Elis, a small man with a wrinkled face, a big nose, big ears and a big smile. Elis chose only the best cod from the local trawlermen, bought only the finest Greek oil, and he fried the best battered cod and chips this side of Offa's Dyke. He was a tenor in the male voice choir, and he entertained his customers while he was frying with selections from Verdi and George Formby, just like Evan Rowlands, the singing butcher, before him. The ladies with their blue rinses dreamed he was singing just for them. The only other employee was Mo (short for Myra), bubbly and blonde from a bottle, with a smile and a song for everyone no matter how down she felt, and left on the shelf on the wrong – or right – side of 40. Mo filleted the fish, prepared the batter to Elis' recipe, and served in the shop. She too sang to the customers – hits from the rock and roll years, Buddy Holly a speciality. They made a good team, Elis the operatic diva with his battered cod special, Mo the rockabilly queen with a lipstick smile, and the big man who used to be a king.

Time passed and word went round the town that this was the best chippie in the land, and while the customers queued, Mo and Elis sang, and the king wrapped their portions in the *Cambrian News*. Best thing in the local paper, they would say. But old Elis was past retiring age and he was enjoying sitting on the park benches singing barbershop quartets with his old schoolmates. More and more, Mo and the king were left to run the shop, and finally the big man realised that he was falling in love with the woman with the breathy valleys voice. He thought of proposing, but he had little money and he thought Mo deserved only the finest gold ring. He had seen one in the window of the jewellers on Dark Gate Street, but it would take him years to save up on the wages that old Elis paid. But save up he did, and the jeweller kept the ring to one side, and for three whole years the king kept his feelings to himself. With the money in his pocket he went to the jewellers and left with the plain but expensive gold ring.

After work that evening, Mo and the king closed up the shop and he walked her back along the seafront, but instead of saying goodnight he escorted her to her door and mumbled that he had long loved her company, how her singing lit a candle in his heart, and how her beautiful face made his life worthwhile. He placed the ring on her finger and he waited. She just stared at the ring, and then said, 'How could you share a shop with me all these years and never say nothin'? I liked you all those years ago, you big oaf. Now, I dunno.' She looked again at the simple plain ring. 'Looks like you got it out of a cracker. Is that all you think of me?' and she took it from her finger and threw it as far as she could into the sea, before turning and slamming the door behind her. The king sat on a bench on the seafront all night with his head down and his collar up, his trousers pecked at by pigeons in the hope of food. That day at work, neither of them spoke; they just got on with their jobs and soon life was back to normal. And more and more customers came to the little chippie on the seafront to hear the songs and sample the quality cod.

One evening, Mo was gutting the fish before battering them when she felt something hard amongst the innards. She held it up in her gloved hand, rinsed it under the tap, and stared at it. It was a gold ring, the very ring that the king had given her, and now she looked at it closely, she could see it wasn't a cheap ring; it shone and it sparkled. She turned and looked at the king, at the big daft man with jet black hair and deep dark eyes, strong, solid, reliable. She stood on tiptoes, put her arms around his neck and kissed him, leaving two red lipstick marks on his cheek. He stared at her, and after a pause he began to sing, in a most beautiful baritone, 'Well, since my baby left me, I found a new place to dwell, down at the end of Darkgate Street, at Heartbreak Hotel,' and he took her by the hand and he took her by the waist and he kissed her on the lips and they jived around that fish and chip emporium all night as he sang everything from 'Are you Lonesome Tonight?' to 'All Shook Up', finishing on 'She Wears My Ring'.

Well, Mo and the king were married, Elis retired and left them the business and every night was like Las Vegas with extra chips. They truly lived happily ever after, and although many in the town suspected who the king really was, no one said a word because they knew that if his secret was blown, there would be no more boogie nights in the old town that night. He was the King of Ceredigion Cod, and that was all he needed. This was all a long time ago, and at the end of the happiest of lives, Mo took his ashes to the rock up in the mountains where he had written his name all those years before and scattered him into the wind. To this day, she takes his brushes, and repaints the words so her king will never be forgotten.

A true story? Well, in 1968 a woman thought she spotted a familiar face driving a big car in Aberystwyth, and told her husband, 'That's the king,' and he saw no reason to disbelieve her. There are some who think that the king was in fact Welsh, from the Preseli Hills. In the 1980s, the legendary King impersonator Peter Singh ran a takeaway in Swansea, sold Love Me Tender Burgers and meals for one called Are You Lonesome Tonight, while singing 'Who's Sari Now' and 'Turbans Over Memphis'. He once recorded 'Blue Suede Shoes' with members of Man, and was photographed with The Clash. The King even has a festival dedicated to him every year in Porthcawl. In 2012 they claimed to have broken a new world record with 814 Kings, the largest gathering of his impersonators in the world.

Still far-fetched? Robert Plant is often seen in Aberystwyth, Bob Dylan is thought to have lived in Llanddewi Brefi, General de Gaulle is said to have led the French Resistance in the early years of the 1940s from an upstairs room on Pier Street, and former President Jimmy Carter was once spotted drinking in the Talbot in Tregaron.

There is a rock on the A44 on the Ceredigion border with the name of the King written upon it, as if welcoming students back to the university in Aberystwyth. It's been there since 1962 when two pranksters wrote the name of a Plaid Cymru candidate, Islwyn Ffowc Elis, on it. It was changed to the King, then to Benny Hill, then Leeds United when they won the League, and back to the King. After someone tried to blow it up, it moved to a nearby rock.

And Ceredigion has another iconic rock, halfway between Aberystwyth and Aberaeron. On the remains of the gable end of a cottage wall is written in large distinctive letters the slogan 'Cofiwch Dryweryn': Remember Tryweryn. It invites reflection on the village and inhabitants of Capel Celyn, flooded deliberately in the 1960s to build Tryweryn Reservoir to supply drinking water to Liverpool. It sparked protests across the land from people who felt that their identity, culture and language were under threat from depopulation, second homes, and lack of jobs. It was a land that needed heroes.

Stories of rocks are everywhere. The National Library of Wales has a secret tunnel that leads to the sea, Aberystwyth has fake bardic standing stones in the middle of the castle and Rhydypennau has severed stone heads, so there seems no reason why Ceredigion shouldn't have its own folk hero, the legendary King of the Rocks, Elfys Preseli.

Notes

Introduction

The quotation by Saunders Lewis comes from 'The Folk Poets' by
W. Rhys Nicholas in the *Writers of Wales* series (ed. Stephens, Meic
& R. Brinley Jones (University of Wales Press and the Welsh Arts
Council, 1978)).

Chapter 1:   Mari Berllan Pitter

Retold from fragments of folk memory which, when pieced
together, tell a very different story to those in newspapers and
books. The ruin of Mari's cottage can still be seen.

Chapter 2:   Sir Dafydd Llwyd,
the Conjurer of Ceredigion

Tales of Sir Dafydd are retold from Edmund Jones and J. Ceredig
Davies. Stories of conjurers can be found in J. Ceredig Davies and
Kate Bosse Griffiths. Folk memory is responsible for the story of
'Dick Spot', 'The National Library' and 'Fagwyr Fawr'. People will
still take you to one side and whisper stories of the *dyn hysbys*, but
it would not be wise to say too much.

Chapter 3:   Tales of the Tylwyth Teg

'Fleet-Footed Sgilti' and 'Elyr the Harpist' are retold from
Myra Evans. 'The Fairy Bride' is from John Sampson. Encounters
with *y tylwyth teg* are still being passed on within families. Stories of

the Irish fairies can be found in Lenihan, Eddie, *Meeting the Other Crowd* (Penguin Group US, 2004)

CHAPTER 4:   JOHN THE PAINTER AND THE FAIRY RING

'Shui Rhys' is retold from Wirt Sikes and J. Ceredig Davies. Einion's Bridge is from J. Ceredig Davies. 'John the Painter' is from Elizabeth Sheppard Jones, Eirwen Jones and more.

CHAPTER 5:   THE ABERYSTWYTH HIRING FAIR

Retold from Eirwen Jones. Another version of the 'Fairy Midwife' story from Swyddyffynnon is in T. Gwynn Jones. Studt's fairs continue to roll into town every November, though the old site of the hiring fair is now a children's playground. Young folk seeking work can still be seen in the doorway of the Angel.

CHAPTER 6:   THE LLWYNWERMWNT CHANGELING

Retold from Myra Evans. The Llwynwermwnt farmhouse and the Nantypele millpond still exist. The story of Bridget Cleary can be found in Bourke, Angela, *The Burning of Bridget Cleary: A True Story* (Random House, 2010).

CHAPTER 7:   THE LADY OF FELIN-WERN MILLPOND

Retold from Myra Evans. Felin-Wern mill and farmhouse still stand, but the millwheel has recently gone and the millpond was filled in fifty years ago.

CHAPTER 8:   THE SALTY WELSH SEA

Retold from Gwyn Jones. The sea is still salty and full of tipsy mermaids.

CHAPTER 9:   RHYSYN AND THE MERMAID

Retold from Myra Evans. Tangeulan still stood in the mid-nineteenth century.

CHAPTER 10: THE PETRIFIED FOREST

Cantre'r Gwaelod first appeared in the thirteenth-century *Black Book of Carmarthen*, in a poem praising Seithennin, a sixth-century hero who died in a flood, and pointing a stern finger of blame at the well maiden Mererid. The story was later popularised in the eighteenth century song 'The Bells of Aberdovey' and the poem, the 'Bells of Cantre'r Gwaelod' from 1869, and has subsequently appeared in countless collections of Welsh stories, TV programmes, books, films and art, and is forever being rewritten to suit our times.

'Plant Rhys Ddwfn' is a folk tale, still in memory in the north, and is also another name for the fairies. It was printed in the first edition of *Brython*, a newspaper, quoted in *Celtic Folklore; Welsh and Manx, Vol.1* (Oxford University Press, 1901) by Sir John Rhys.

'Nodon's Well' is from Myra Evans, and Craig Aderyn is still a breeding ground for birds.

CHAPTER 11: THE TALE OF TALIESIN

The *Book of Taliesin* is a collection of poems written down in the early fourteenth century. Taliesin is thought to have been a mixture of sixth-century court poet, bard and singer; maybe a storyteller; or maybe many poets from different eras, a folk memory. There are many books on his poetry and lives, yet his story is unclear, making him the perfect folk hero. The version here is a compilation of current folk tales and one written out in a school exercise book by Dyfed Lloyd Evans of the Celtnet website. The second story is from the writings of Glasynys, the novelist and poet Owen Wynne Jones, retold by Sir John Rhys.

CHAPTER 12: THE OLD TOAD OF BORTH BOG

Retold from Elisabeth Sheppard-Jones. The oldest animals appeared in Thomas Williams of Trefriw, who recorded it in 1594, retold by George Borrow. 'The Old Hag' is in Evan Isaac, and from the memory and telling of storyteller Anthony Morris.

CHAPTER 13: DAFYDD MEURIG AND
THE DANCING BEAR

Retold from Bernard Henderson and Steven Jones and T. Gwynn
Jones. Owain Lawgoch at Gilfach yr Halen Cave is from Myra Evans.
Owain Lawgoch, or Owen of the Red Hand, was one of the last
Welsh princes.

CHAPTER 14: THE WICKEDEST MAN IN CEREDIGION

This story is inherently true, though embellished with folk
memory. Sir Herbert's excesses had already become folk tales during
his lifetime. History says he died in bed, but folk memory insists
he shot himself. Bethan Phillips has written the full story of the
house in *Peterwell: History of a Mansion and its Infamous Squire*
(Cymdeithas Lyfrau Ceredigion, 1997).

CHAPTER 15: TWM SIÔN CATI,
THE TREGARON TRICKSTER

Stories of Twm are well known in folk memory, and have been
documented in an unpublished thesis by M.R.E. Thomas, and by
the Twm of today, Dafydd Wyn Morgan. He has appeared in
animated films, TV series and strip cartoons. Little is known
about Siôn Cwilt, and the stories come from folk memory and the
writing of T. Llew Jones.

CHAPTER 16: THE GREEN MAN OF NO MAN'S LAND

Retold from John Sampson. Information on the Wood family
comes from Eldra and A.O.H. Jarman in *The Welsh Gypsies:
Children of Abram Wood* (University of Wales Press, 2001),
and Tom MacDonald told the story of Johnnie MacDonald in
The White Lanes of Summer.

CHAPTER 17: THE WAR OF THE LITTLE ENGLISHMAN

The full story has been documented by Eirian Jones. Ask anyone on
Mynydd Bach if they know any stories, and this is the one they will
tell. It is a story from history that has become a folk tale, sometimes
embellished, sometimes imperfectly remembered, sometimes

memorised, and sometimes just known. The story anticipates the Rebecca Riots by a quarter of a century, when men also dressed as women to fight the injustice of road toll charges. Cross-dressing is a common expression of subversion in folk cultures across the world.

CHAPTER 18: THE DEVIL'S BRIDGE

'The Devil in Llanarth Church Tower' is in J. Ceredig Davies and Myra Evans; 'The Devil's Black Ring' is from Myra Evans; the 'Ladies of Llanddewi Brefi Church' is in J. Ceredig Davies; 'Sir Dafydd's Soul' is in J. Ceredig Davies; 'The Devil's Footprints' is from folk memory; the story of 'The Devil's Bridge' is in every book, tourist guide, and on an information board in the village; 'The Devil's Stone' is from folk memory and in E.R. Horsfall-Turner, and 'Plant Mat' is in George Borrow and folk memory.

CHAPTER 19: THE HEADLESS DOG OF PENPARCAU

'Maelor and His Sons' is retold from the sixteenth-century writings of Siôn Dafydd Rhys, via T. Gwynn Jones and Chris Grooms. 'The Headless Dog' is still told as a folk tale in the area, and appears in Llowarch, *More Weird Wonders of Wales* (Churchwarden Publications, 1989). 'The Faithful Sheepdog' is from a handwritten manuscript amongst Myra Evans' papers. Stories of the Cwn Annwn and the Beast of Bont are commonly found in folk memory and the press.

CHAPTER 20: THE TRANSVESTITE WHITE LADY
OF BROGINAN

Most of the encounters with ghosts are from current folk memory, oral tales, books and websites. 'The White Lady' is in Richard Holland, 'Siaci Clifforch' is from Myra Evans and Marie Trevelyan, and the remainder are from folk memory.

CHAPTER 21: CROOKED BETI GRWCA

'Beti Grwca', 'The Bogey' and 'Guto' are retold from Myra Evans, and are all set within a few miles of each other. There is still a bridge over the Rhyd, though Gilfach yr Halen is now a holiday village. The Hafod *Bwca* is from a mixture of folk memory and printed snippets. The grounds are open to the public, though the house is long gone.

CHAPTER 22: SIGL-DI-GWT

Retold from Myra Evans. This story and 'The Cobbler and the Red Mannikin' bear a resemblance to two Grimm's Tales; 'Rumpelstiltskin' and 'The Elves and the Shoemaker'. No one else in New Quay appears to know them, which suggests they are forgotten or were only known within Myra's family or friends. The Brothers Grimm themselves collected tales from family, friends and servants, and within a limited geographical area. Sir John Rhys discusses other Welsh versions of 'Sigl-di-gwt'. Myra translates Sigl-di-gwt as 'Shake my Tail', although Sigl-di-gwt is the name for the Wagtail. Here is a translation of the lullaby, courtesy of Elsa Davies:

My dear little baby, the best in the world,
How would I live at all without your company?
As I love you, my innocent baby!
You are my treasure, the pleasure of your mam.

Lullaby, lullaby, sleep gently now
You will have dreams about birds and lambs
Flowers, and little sweet things in the country
Lullaby, sleep before your dad comes.

My dear little baby, most beautiful in the country,
Your mami's love, and your father's treasure,
You are my dearest one, my gentle little baby
And in your person, joins every charm.

Lullaby, lullaby, comfortable be your slumber
Mam is watching you, your dearest face
Angels will be your watch, don't give one whimper
Lullaby, rest quietly and gently.

My dear little baby the most beautiful in being
Sleep while your mami is twisting at the wheel
Close your eyes, and take your sleep.
Sleep you quietly while you are on my lap.

There! I see that sleep has come
Lullaby, lullaby, I will go to my wheel
Sleep now comfortably, your mam will be watching
Lullaby, lullaby, you'll not have any harm.

Chapter 23: The Ffos y Ffin Goblin and the One-Eyed Preacher

The Ffos y Ffin Goblin is from Myra Evans, and who knows what it would have made of the noise of the heavy lorries racing past the Red Lion now. Henllan has been documented by John Meirion Jones. The remaining stories are from folk memory. The description of the priest's visit to the Otherworld is in J. Ceredig Davies.

Chapter 24: The Brwcsod of Ffair Rhos

The tale of the *Brwcsod* is from folk memory and a story told by Mary Davies of Ffair Rhos to Robin Gwyndaf on 4 May 1979. The Hanged Man is well documented in both print and folk memory, and the orcs and goblins of Llywernog is a folk tale in gestation.

Chapter 25: The Talking Tree of Cwmystwyth

'The Talking Tree' is from Llowarch, 'The Three Sisters' from folk memory, 'The Tail of the White Mare' from T. Gwynn Jones, 'Hen Gell' is retold from Myra Evans, and 'The Black Stallion' from a handwritten manuscript by Myra Evans.

Chapter 26: The Dribbling Cow and Other Curious Cattle

'The Three Roan Calves' and 'The Dribbling Cow' were told by Kate Davies to Robin Gwyndaf at Pren-gwyn near Llandysul on 16 June 1973. They were told to Mrs Davies by her Aunt Kitty.

Both are in the Robin Gwyndaf collection at St Fagans. 'The Three Roan Calves' also appears in Kate Davies's book *Hafau fy Mhlentyndod Ym Mhentref Pren-Gwyn* (Gwasg Gomer, 1970). The Ychen Bannog still exist in folk memory, and the story of 'The Fairy Cattle' of Llyn Eiddwen is from folk memory.

CHAPTER 27: THE ELEPHANT THAT DIED IN TREGARON

The story exists strongly in folk memory, and has been researched and written down by Mary-Ann Constantine. The recent archaeological dig has only served to fuel the folk tale.

CHAPTER 28: THE QUEER COUPLE WHO ALWAYS QUARRELLED

The tale of the Queer Couple is in the David Thomas Collection at the National Library of Wales; 'The Old Miser' is from Llowarch; 'Siani Pob Man' is from Myra Evans and folk memory; 'The Strongest Man' is from from David Gorman, 'The Strongest Man in Aberystwyth' in the *Dyfed Family History Journal*, Vol.5 No.4, August 1995; information on Joseph Jenkins comes from his own *Diary of a Welsh Swagman 1869 to 1894*, and the remaining stories are from folk memory. Cardi jokes are told everywhere.

CHAPTER 29: JULIE'S BEEN WORKING FOR THE DRUGS SQUAD

Most of these stories are contemporary tales still simmering in a Ceredigion cauldron, flavoured by occasionally accurate newspaper reports and a little seasoning of truth and mischief. Lyn Ebeneezer has documented the story of Operation Julie.

CHAPTER 30: THE KING OF THE ROCKS

Pieced together from folk memory and oral tales. There are tales of Elvis running a chip shop in Aberystwyth, and the story of 'The Fish and the Ring' is a well-known fishy tail from Aber, as well as elsewhere around Wales. Everything else is absolutely true. Promise.

BIBLIOGRAPHY

Borrow, George, *Wild Wales: Its People, Language and Scenery* (London: Woodfall and Kinder, 1862)

Constantine, Mary-Ann, *The Breathing* (Aberystwyth: Planet, 2008).

Davies, Jonathan Ceredig, *Folk-Lore of West and Mid-Wales* (Aberystwyth: Welsh Gazette, 1911)

Davies, Llinos M., *Crochan Ceredigion* (Aberystwyth: Cwmdeithas Lyfrau Ceredigion, 1992)

Enoch, Randall Evans, *Llanfihangel Genau'r Glyn – the History of a Community* (Llandre: Wendall Publishing, 2010)

Evans, Caradoc, *My People* (London: Andrew Melrose, 1915)

Evans, Hugh, *Y Tylwyth Teg* (Liverpool: Hugh Evans, 1935)

Evans, Myra, *Casgliad o Chwedlau Newydd* (Aberystwyth: *Cambrian News*, 1926)

Evans, Myra, *Atgofion Ceinewydd* (Aberystwyth: Cymdeithas Lyfrau Ceredigion, 1961)

Evans, D. Silvan & John Jones, *Ysten Siôned* (Wrexham: Hughes A'l Fab, 3rd edition, 1892)

Gerald of Wales, *The Journey Through Wales and the Description of Wales* (London: Penguin Classics, 1978)

Griffiths, Kate Bosse, *Byd y Dyn Hysbys: Swyngyfaredd yng Nghymru* (Talybont, Y Lolfa, 1977)

Grooms, Chris, *The Giants of Wales: Cewri Cymru* (Cardiff: Edwin Mellen Press Ltd, 1993)

Gwyndaf, Robin, *Welsh Folk Tales/Chwedlau Gwerin Cymru* (Cardiff: National Museum of Wales, 1989)

Henderson, Bernard and Stephen Jones, *Wonder Tales of Ancient Wales* (London: Philip Allan & Co., 1921)

Holland, Richard, *Haunted Wales: A Guide to Welsh Ghostlore* (Stroud: The History Press, 2011)

Horsfall-Turner, E.R., *Walks and Wanderings in County Cardigan* (Llanidloes: Thomas Harrison & Sons, 1902)

Howells, W., *Cambrian Superstitions* (London: Tipton, 1831)

Isaac, Evan, *Coelion Cymru* (Aberystwyth: Y Clwb Llyfrau Cymreig, 1938)

Jarman, Eldra and A.O.H. Jarman, *The Welsh Gypsies: Children of Abraham Wood* (Cardiff: University of Wales Press, 1991)

Jenkins, J. Geraint, *Life and Tradition in Rural Wales* (London: Dent, 1976)

Jones, Edmund, *The Appearance of Evil: Apparitions of Spirits in Wales* (Cardiff: University of Wales Press, 2003)

Jones, Eirian, *The War of the Little Englishman: Enclosure Riots on a Lonely Welsh Hillside* (Talybont: Y Lolfa, 2007)

Jones, Eirwen, *Folk Tales of Wales* (Edinburgh: Thomas Nelson, 1947).

Jones, Gwyn, *Welsh Legends and Folk-Tales* (Oxford: Oxford University Press, 1955)

Jones, Margaret, *It Came, To Pass* (Caerleon: Apecs Press, 2007)

Jones, Noragh, *Cwmrheidol People* (Aberystwyth: Pilgrim Press, 2008)

Jones, T. Gwynn, *Welsh Folklore & Folk-custom* (London: Methuen, 1930)

Llowarch, *More Weird Wonders of Wales* (Aberystwyth: Churchwarden Publications, 1989)

MacDonald, Tom, *The White Lanes of Summer* (London: Macmillan, 1975)

Meyrick, Samuel Rush, *The History and Antiquities of the County of Cardigan* (London: Longman, Hurst, Rees and Orme, 1810)

Morgan, Gerald, *Ceredigion: A Wealth of History* (Llandysul: Gwasg Gomer, 2005)

Nicholas, W. Rhys, *The Folk Poets* (Cardiff: University of Wales Press, 1978)

Owen, Elias, *Welsh Folk-lore: a Collection of the Folk Tales and Legends of North Wales* (Woodall, Minshall and Company, 1896)

Parry-Jones, D., *Welsh Children's Games and Pastimes* (Denbigh:

Gee & Son, 1964)

— *Welsh Legends and Fairy Lore* (London: BT Batsford Ltd, 1953)

Phillips, Bethan, *The Lovers' Graves: 6 True Tales that Shocked Wales*
(Llandysul: Gomer Press, 2007)

— *Pity the Swagman* (Aberystwyth: Cymdeithas Lyfrau
Ceredigion Gyf, 2002)

Rhys, Sir John, *Celtic Folklore: Welsh and Manx, Vol 1.* (Oxford:
Clarendon Press, 1891)

Ross, Anne, *Folklore of Wales* (Stroud: NPI Media Group, 2001)

Sampson, John, *XXI Welsh Gypsy Folk-Tales* (Newtown: Gregynog
Press, 1933)

Sheppard-Jones, Elisabeth, *Welsh Legendary Tales*, (London:
Nelson, 1959)

Sikes, Wirt, 'The Realm of Faerie', *British Goblins: Welsh Folk
Lore, Fairy Mythology, Legends and Traditions* (London:
J.R. Osgood and Company, 1880)

Suggett, Richard, *A History of Magic and Witchcraft in Wales*
(Stroud: The History Press, 2008)

Thomas, W. Jenkyn, *The Welsh Fairy Book* (London: A&C
Black Ltd, 1938)

Thorne, David, *Chwedlau Gwerin Glannau Teifi*
(Llandysul: Gwasg Gomer, 1981)

Trevelyan, Marie, *Folk-lore and Folk Stories of Wales*
(London: Elliot Stock, 1909)

MANUSCRIPTS

Myra Evans' papers courtesy of Iola Billings

Thomas, David, Papers in National Library of Wales, 1924

Thomas, M.R.E., 'Twm Siôn Cati: Truth, Tales and Tradition',
(unpublished thesis, 2003)

The 'Susan Passmore Collection' in Ceredigion Government Archive

The 'Robin Gwyndaf Collection' in St Fagans Archive at the
National Museum of Wales

WEBSITES

Evans, Dyfed Lloyd, Celtnet http://www.celtnet.org.uk/

If you enjoyed this book, you may also be interested in …

Pembrokeshire Folk Tales

CHRISTINE WILLISON

Pembrokeshire is home to a rich and diverse collection of tales. Mermaids and pirates roam the county's spectacular coastline; the frightful Anfanc terrorises the village of Brynberian and captivating princesses have been kidnapped from Cilgerran Castle. Christine Willison explores the county, along with some beautiful illustrations and a mysterious companion …

978 0 7524 6565 4

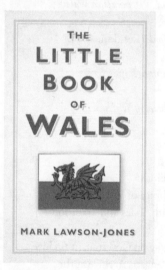

The Little Book of Wales

MARK LAWSON-JONES

Discover the real Wales, with all its unusual crimes and punishments, eccentric inhabitants and famous sons and daughters. This little book is full of authentically bizarre bits of historic trivia, with each read revealing something new about the people, the heritage, the secrets and the enduring fascination of Wales.

978 0 7524 8927 8

Visit our website and discover thousands of other History Press books.

www.thehistorypress.co.uk